Marijuana

Recent Titles in
Contributions in Criminology and Penology

MARIJUANA

Costs of Abuse, Costs of Control

Mark A. R. Kleiman

CONTRIBUTIONS IN CRIMINOLOGY AND PENOLOGY,
NUMBER 22

GREENWOOD PRESS
New York
Westport, Connecticut
London

Library of Congress Cataloging-in-Publication Data

Kleiman, Mark A. R.
  Marijuana : costs of abuse, costs of control / Mark A. R. Kleiman.
    p. cm. — (Contributions in criminology and penology, ISSN
  0732–4464 : no. 22)
    Bibliography: p.
    Includes index.
    ISBN 0–313–25853–8 (lib. bdg. : alk. paper)
    1. Marihuana—United States.   2. Narcotics, Control of—United
  States.   I. Title.   II. Series.
  HV5822.M3K53   1989
  362.2′9—dc19   88–7712

British Library Cataloguing in Publication Data is available.

Library of Congress Catalog Card Number: 88–7712
ISBN: 0–313–25853–8
ISSN: 0732–4464

First published in 1989

Greenwood Press, Inc.
88 Post Road West, Westport, Connecticut   06881

Printed in the United States of America

∞

The paper used in this book complies with the
Permanent Paper Standard issued by the National
Information Standards Organization (Z39.48–1984).

10 9 8 7 6 5 4 3 2

For John Kaplan

Contents

Tables and Graphs

Preface

This book is about how to choose policies. Its particular focus is choosing among alternative ways of enforcing the marijuana laws at the federal level. Its commitment is less to a conclusion than to a method: the systematic enumeration of goals and the evaluation of alternatives in light of their likely results.

Historians have the benefit of hindsight (in Greek, epimetheus), and make a profession of being wise after the event. Policy makers and their advisers need foresight (prometheus), a notoriously less reliable tool; chained to the rock of what they have done and can no longer change, they are gnawed at by the vulture of regret.

It would be bad enough to act in a known present on an unknown future. In fact, even the present is more guessed at than known. Macroeconomic managers at least have the luxury of current data on wages and prices, unemployment and capacity utilization; most policy makers have to make do with what is known now about conditions one, two, or three years ago.

In 1981 and 1982, I thought about marijuana policy from the perspective of a new administration pledged to a war on drugs. I tried to calculate how an increase in resources would serve the twin goals of reducing abuse and limiting the power and wealth of large criminal organizations. (At that point, I was working with 1979 data.) My conclusions were discouraging.

A major increase in enforcement came about nevertheless; thus there is now experience to compare with those predictions. The strategy of the present volume is to reproduce the analysis from the perspective of 1982 (using 1982 data) and to compare results (up to 1985–1986, after which the data peter out) with expectations. (Not to hold the reader in unbearable suspense, the answer is that results match expectations pretty well, but not perfectly.)

The point is not to second-guess what was done and cannot be recalled, but rather to suggest how such choices ought to be made in the future. It is frustrating not to have, even now, the current data on which a comprehensive judgment of the policy decisions of 1982 might be based, but that is the nature of the beast. While fresher information might lead to different judgments, there is no suggestion in scattered more recent reports that would require a fundamental rethinking.

Acknowledgments

I began to do the thinking and calculations that went into the current volume as a drug policy analyst in the Office of Policy and Management Analysis of the Criminal Division, U.S. Department of Justice. Stephen B. Hitchner, Jr., founding director of that office, was generous with moral and bureaucratic support, with gentle pressure not to settle for "almost right," and with tough, helpful criticism. My colleagues in OPMA tolerated my work habits and my sense of humor and produced work that made me look good during my tenure as director. Alexander H. Williams, III, Chief of the Criminal Division's Narcotic and Dangerous Drug Section, offered friendship and lively interest when organizational and professional pressures would have suggested a distant hostility. Bruce Peterson, Special Assistant to the Deputy Assistant Attorney General for Narcotics and Organized Crime, was a faithful colleague and comrade-in-arms in the battle to use the results of policy analysis to help shape drug enforcement and prosecution programs. Philip B. Heymann and D. Lowell Jensen, successively Assistant Attorneys General in charge of the Criminal Division, had the ingenuity to create a capacity for policy analysis in an organization dominated by lawyers and the courage to maintain that capacity in a climate increasingly hostile to anything but unreflective support for an ideologically determined "line."

It was Phil Heymann, once again, who found space, money, and a title for me at the Center for Criminal Justice of Harvard Law School so that I could start the process of turning a mass of memos into a sustained argument. In that enterprise I would like to thank Mark H. Moore, Thomas C. Schelling, Daniel Meltzer, and John Kaplan. Mark Moore also provided a new organizational home, at the Program in Criminal Justice Policy and Management of the John F. Kennedy School of Government. Additional thanks are due to K. C. Sheehan, Dan Rosenbaum, Elizabeth Chen, Suzanne Forbis, and (most of all) Lesley K. Friedman; they found the footnotes, fixed the grammar, and typed the drafts. When their work was done, Susanna Kaysen went through and cleaned up the prose. The process of converting that argument into the present book began with a suggestion from Mildred Vasan of Greenwood Press, and has continued with her patient support. The extensive revisions required could not have been accomplished without the invaluable assistance of Aaron Saiger and Jessica Avery. Saul Weingart read and commented on a late draft.

My greatest personal debt is to Newell B. Mack, without whose unrelenting friendly pressure and unwavering support I might have given up a dozen times. I doubt that my many obligations to him ever could have been repaid; his premature death deprived me and countless others of many things, of which the opportunity for repayment was the least.

My greatest creditor intellectually is Peter Reuter, with whom I have been trading telephone calls and drafts since 1979. We have been collaborating so long and so closely that it is no longer possible to determine precisely which ideas are whose. Mere footnoting cannot express how much of this product is his.

Introduction: The Issue and the Argument

How, and how vigorously, should U.S. federal law enforcement agencies enforce the laws against dealing in marijuana? The answer depends in part—but only in part—on one's view of the relative importance of the two distinct problems associated with marijuana.

The first of these is the problem of marijuana consumption. Marijuana is used more or less regularly by some 20 million Americans.[1] Some 10 or 20 percent of them smoke enough to remain under the drug's influence for a large fraction of all their waking hours. Millions of marijuana users, including hundreds of thousands of heavy daily users, are adolescents.[2] While the extent to which these facts constitute bad news is a matter of some debate (see chapter 1), they are seen by many as profoundly worrying indicators of a major social problem.

The other problem associated with marijuana is marijuana dealing. Along with dealing in heroin and cocaine, it is one of the nation's three richest illicit markets, accounting annually for several billion dollars in criminal revenue.[3] The illicit market also generates violent crimes and creates wealthy and powerful criminals and criminal organizations. Violence and criminal wealth and power represent two challenges to a society ruled by its laws.

Neither the drug abuse problem nor the illicit-market problem is a small one. Moreover, a policy beneficial from the perspective of one problem might be detrimental from the perspective of the other. Legalization, for example, though it would solve the criminal-market problem at a stroke, would very likely increase the number of heavy smokers. By contrast, a marijuana cartel, if one existed, would restrict quantity, raise price, and thus reduce consumption; but such a cartel would be rich, violent, corrupting, and dangerous.[4]

Even limiting consideration to the narrower range of possible enforcement policies under a continuing marijuana ban, as this book will largely do, there is still tension between the two goals. Enforcement strategies that effectively reduce supply can exacerbate the problems of criminal wealth, violence, and corruption. Success in reducing marijuana consumption can also worsen drug abuse overall by inducing consumers to seek substitutes, some of which might be more dangerous than their initial choice. The best enforcement strategy overall will be the one that minimizes the sum of the two costs of marijuana: the cost of drug abuse and the cost imposed by criminal markets.

Neither facts nor value judgments alone suffice to answer the question, "What is the best policy?" The answer depends both on how one views the relative gravity of the two problems and on how drug abuse and the drug markets behave when confronted with various enforcement strategies.

Most of this book is concerned with the second question: How will the markets change if enforcement is increased? Its conclusion is pessimistic. Any feasible increase in federal enforcement will produce only slight and severely qualified benefits from the point of view of drug abuse. Federal enforcement can influence conditions in the marijuana market only with great difficulty. Higher prices will cause consumers to cut back only modestly on marijuana smoking while simultaneously encouraging use of more potent forms of marijuana and the use of other, still more dangerous, drugs.

At the same time, increasing enforcement will worsen the illicit-market problem. The marijuana market will become significantly more lucrative, and a larger share of increased illicit revenues will go to particularly criminal and violent individuals and organizations.

This conclusion rests broadly on the following argument, supported by the actual experience of the 1980s.

There is an effectively unlimited supply of imported marijuana in the farmer's field at low prices. Importing and distributing the drug requires no special skills. Therefore, *shortages* of marijuana—circumstances in which consumers cannot find any of the drug at something close to the going price—are likely to be infrequent and highly localized.

Federal enforcement's efforts to reduce consumption are therefore entirely mediated by price: the measure of success is the magnitude of shifts of the supply curve.

Moving the supply curve, however, is a weapon of limited power. Even a doubling of 1986 federal enforcement levels, which are themselves 50 percent higher than the 1982 levels, would increase the price of marijuana to the consumer by only about 25 percent over the 1982 price. Since marijuana already accounts for about a third of federal drug enforcement resources, a doubling would require a very substantial resource reallocation. At the same time, marijuana consumption would decline only modestly as prices rose, because the drug is inexpensive relative to consumers' budgets and relative to the prices of substitutes.

Thus, even vigorous feasible enforcement efforts would produce only slight benefits in drug abuse control, whose value would be offset by the substitution of higher-potency marijuana, hallucinogens, or inhalants for the low-potency imported marijuana made more expensive by enforcement efforts.

In the criminal market, an increased price without a significant consumption decrease will raise total revenue. If it were true that the social costs of an illicit market rose proportionately with total revenues, this would already be a bad deal. In fact, strengthened enforcement is also likely to give an advantage to tightly organized firms able to wield violence and corruption effectively, since such firms are the most enforcement-resistant. To the extent that this is so, tightened enforcement will be a double loser on the criminal-markets side: it will give the worst of the bad guys an increasing share of a bigger revenue pie.

This analysis supports both a reduction in federal marijuana enforcement efforts and their redirection towards the most violent dealing groups. At the very least, the doubling in that effort since the early 1980s, which has proven every bit as ineffective as could have been expected, ought to be reversed. The most federal enforcement can do is to prevent "effective decriminalization," or the point at which marijuana trafficking is so open and flagrant that demand for the drug increases because the apparent social disapproval is reduced.

As an operational matter, it would be fairly easy to cut back selectively on marijuana enforcement by cutting into the drug interdiction budgets of the Coast Guard and Customs service and by revising the Drug Enforcement Administration (DEA) target evaluation system to downgrade the importance attached to marijuana dealers. Remaining enforcement activity should be directed toward the most violent and corrupting organizations. Operationally, this means calculating the importance of individual marijuana cases primarily according to their nondrug elements, rather than drug volumes.

In sum, the combined results of increased enforcement—only marginal benefit on the drug-abuse side and a significantly less attractive illicit market situation—lead to the conclusion that a lowering of enforcement levels (although not necessarily the elimination of enforcement) is the most desirable policy available. Halving the current federal marijuana enforcement budget could save $320 million in expenditures and free prison cells for other offenders, reduce the earnings of marijuana dealers and the drug budgets of marijuana users by 2 percent, and increase marijuana consumption by only 1.5 percent.[5]

The arguments in favor of reduced enforcement do not apply directly to the question of legalization. Legalization's effects on the market would go well beyond the impact of merely decreasing enforcement levels. There are already a few million problem marijuana users (assuming that anyone who smokes an average of five or more joints per day has a problem). It is possible that legalization would increase this total by very little, but there is no way of knowing in advance. It is also possible that legalization could double the number of people—largely young people—who are under the influence of marijuana for virtually all of their waking hours. This is not a pleasant prospect. Nor, as a practical matter, could we try legalization just as an experiment. Legalization would be very difficult and very expensive to reverse, since the expanded market would present a very difficult enforcement target.

Anyone who has tried his hand at policy analysis will appreciate how much more complicated the world is than our models of it, and how likely the unexpected is to upset the most straightforward predictions. I first developed the argument summarized above between 1981 and 1983, at the end of my tenure as a drug policy analyst for the Department of Justice. I was then attempting to calculate prospectively the effects of the great increase underway in federal marijuana enforcement efforts. Those effects have been more substantial, though not necessarily more beneficial, than I expected.

The chapters that follow thus take a double perspective: that of 1982, looking forward and "predicting" the effects of the policy actually followed, and that of the present, looking back and trying to learn from that experience.

Part I, "The Marijuana Problem," identifies what is at stake in marijuana consumption and dealing, attempts to quantify the size of the problem, and discusses the criteria with which to judge a policy recommendation. Part II, "Choosing a Marijuana Policy," develops a theory of drug dealing and its response to varying levels of enforcement pressure and applies that theory to the early years of the increased federal anti-marijuana enforcement effort of the 1980s. Part III, "Evaluating Marijuana Policy," evaluates that effort and discusses the policy options available for the future.

NOTES

1. National Institute of Drug Abuse, *Population Projections Based on the National Survey on Drug Abuse, 1982* (Washington: Department of Health and Human Services, 1983), table 1A, p. 5.

2. L. D. Johnston, J. G. Bachman, and P. M. O'Malley, *National Trends in Drug Use and Related Factors Among American High School Students and Young Adults, 1975–1986* (Washington: National Institute on Drug Abuse, 1987). Also Johnston et al., "Summary of 1987 Drug Study Results," University of Michigan Press Release, 13 Jan. 1988.

3. J. Michael Polich, Phyllis L. Ellickson, Peter Reuter, and James P. Kahan, *Strategies for Controlling Adolescent Drug Use* (Santa Monica, Cal.: RAND Corporation, 1984), table L8, p. 40.

4. Thomas C. Schelling, *Choice and Consequence* (Cambridge, Mass.: Harvard University Press, 1984).

5. This is discussed more thoroughly in chapter 12.

Part 1
THE MARIJUANA PROBLEM

1

The Marijuana Consumption Problem

Why is marijuana consumption a problem and how serious a problem is it?

At first glance, this seems to be a question for citizens and legislators, one that law enforcement agencies can regard as solved. Marijuana is a problem because Congress has chosen to make it a problem: its manufacture, distribution, and possession are illegal, and it is the function of law enforcement to suppress illegal activity and punish those who engage in it.

But Congress has also chosen, from fiscal prudence or fear of an excessive level of law enforcement intrusion into civil life, to deny federal law enforcement agencies the budgets they would need to enforce vigorously all the laws, all the time, everywhere. That there will be offenses, and even unpunished offenses, is a given. One of the objectives in managing enforcement resources is to minimize the social harms done by those violations that enforcement fails to deter or otherwise prevent. This implies some sort of judgment about which violations cause more harm and which cause less. No consensus exists, however, on the extent of harm caused by marijuana.

In the view of the opponents of marijuana consumption, marijuana damages its users, or at least some of them. Furthermore, it causes users to damage others, or to do less good than they otherwise would to others and to the country at large. Smoking marijuana is also an unconventional (or at least un-

traditional) form of behavior. It is linked, causally or acciden-
tally, in fact or merely in the minds of some citizens, with other
sorts of unconventional, untraditional, or harmful behavior,
including the use of other drugs.

Each marijuana smoker whose smoking is not absolutely
secret also contributes to the marijuana smoking of others, if
only by example. Decisions about the use of psychoactives, like
decisions about what clothes to wear, are influenced by fashion.
Each eighth-grader, in deciding whether and how often to use
marijuana, will be influenced by the number of other eighth-
graders (and ninth-graders) already doing so. If marijuana use
were entirely benign, this effect could not independently serve
as an argument for its suppression. But if marijuana use is bad
for even a fraction of its users this fashion effect (sometimes
misleadingly described as "contagion"[1]) contributes to costs of
consumption and thus to the benefits of suppression.

On the other hand, in the eyes of many of its current and
former consumers, marijuana is a source of harmless recreation
and even of self-improvement, which causes them to be more
creative, social, and tolerant of others than they would have
been had they not become users.[2] Furthermore, marijuana may
be a substitute for other, more hazardous recreations, including
other drugs.

From the viewpoint of law enforcement decision makers, the
legislative ban on the appropriation of funds to enforce it can
be taken as an authoritative determination that, on the balance, the social impact of marijuana is harmful. This does not
exclude the possibility that some marijuana consumption may
be harmless, or at least relatively so. It would not be the only
instance of an activity so dangerous to some that it is banned
for all, though some or even most might engage in it without
suffering or causing harm.

CRITERIA FOR EVALUATING MARIJUANA ABUSE

Types and Perception of Harm

To judge whether and to what extent marijuana is harmful,
we should first refine our notion of "harm." Marijuana might
harm its users, or cause them to damage others, in four ways:

1. *Physical* harm is damage to physical health, for example, reduction in lung capacity.

2. *Psychological* harm is damage to mental health or intellectual capacity of the sort that might be measured by personality profiles or IQ tests.

3. *Motivational* costs include reduction in users' capacity or willingness to achieve their own goals or to carry out their family, social, economic, and civic responsibilities. This might be due to spending excessive or inappropriate periods under the influence of marijuana, or to decreases in capacity or drive lasting beyond the immediate period of drug consumption.

4. Possible *behavioral* effects include intoxicated behavior that is risky or damaging to self or others which the user, if sober, would resist. Driving under the influence illustrates this problem in two ways: intoxication renders the inebriate unfit to drive, and at the same time reduces his ability to perceive that unfitness and to make decisions based on the consequences of driving while incapacitated.

Even when abstract categories of harm have been defined, detecting and measuring harm can still be less than straightforward. Damage done by marijuana use might be noticed in four ways:

1. *Users* might perceive harm to themselves, either contemporaneously with their drug use, in retrospect, or in alternating intervals. A user perceiving harm contemporaneously might quit, choose not to quit because of perceived offsetting benefits, or be unable to quit due to problems of self-command.[3]

2. Users' *intimates and acquaintances*, with emotional or material stakes in particular users' well-being or ability to carry out their responsibilities—parents, mates, children, friends, employers, co-workers, employees, classmates, teachers, physicians, clergy, fellow citizens—might notice effects the user does not.[4]

3. *The scientific community* might measure statistical harm even though it cannot be observed or separated from background levels in individuals; or harm might be measured under laboratory conditions and the results projected onto user populations. Small reductions in mean IQ or slight effects on resistance to disease might be discovered in this way. Similarly, those who encounter people in trouble or causing trouble—police, social workers, crisis inter-

vention workers of various kinds—might notice an overrepresentation of marijuana users among their clients. Most kinds of social harm, such as increases in criminality, will be perceived in these ways if at all.

4. Finally, harm might *not be perceived or measured at all*, as some of the most important health effects of tobacco smoking remained unknown even after smoking and health became a topic of concern.

Furthermore, even if all the forms of marijuana-related *harm* were fully perceived and well measured, the existence of a marijuana consumption *problem*—a situation calling for public or private intervention—would still depend on many other factors: the benefits, if any, of marijuana use; which of the harms were avoidable and at what cost; whether these costs and benefits were going to the same groups; the extent to which marijuana consumption decisions were being made on the basis of adequate information; and so on. One would also want to distinguish between thinking of marijuana use in itself as a problem—as one thinks of PCP (phenylcyclidine or "angel dust") or heroin use, or jumping off bridges, as problems which in themselves virtually entail their consequences—and thinking of "problem users" of marijuana, as one thinks of problem users of alcohol or sleeping pills, or of problem drivers.

The Scarcity of Data

These more subtle questions barely arise in practice, because many of the relevant observations, even the simplest, have not been made. Although there have been numerous laboratory studies of the psychophysiology of consuming either natural cannabis or its primary active ingredient (delta–9-tetrahydrocannabinol, or THC), and extensive sample surveys of marijuana consumption habits, no one has attempted to measure the population health effects of current American levels of cannabis use, nor have there been any cohort or case control studies of the effects of years rather than months of marijuana smoking. There is no survey evidence about the beliefs of users or their associates about the harms being done by marijuana to themselves or the users they know (as opposed to attitude/

opinion questions about marijuana in the abstract). Questions like, "On balance, are you happy or unhappy that you started smoking marijuana?" or, "If you had the decision to make again, would you start smoking marijuana?" have not been asked of a random sample of current and former users. Other questions along the same lines might be:

• Did you ever feel that you were smoking too much?
• If you are a current user, did you ever try to quit?
• If so, how much trouble did you have in quitting?
• If you could quit cold today, would you do so?

Even if such questions had been asked, interpreting the answers would be tricky. Asking a thirty-five-year-old who smoked marijuana when he was in college whether smoking marijuana was a good or bad thing for him may elicit more information about his current political beliefs and his attitudes toward his youth than about the effects of the drug. Asking parents about their children's drug consumption might be equally unilluminating for similar reasons.

There have also been no serious studies of the effects of marijuana-smoking behavior on school or job performance, career development, family formation, or other substantial life events. Such studies would face the difficult task of disentangling the consequences of marijuana use from its mere correlates. The failure to undertake them, however, may result more from the bias of National Institute on Drug Abuse towards biomedical research than from a careful judgment about what kinds of new knowledge could contribute to sensible public choices.

BIOMEDICAL RESEARCH

Despite the large number of published studies on marijuana and health, scientific evaluation of the damage caused by marijuana is highly equivocal. There have been two major review efforts in recent years. In 1982, a study committee of the Institute of Medicine issued a report summarizing the work in the field until that time.[5] Two years later, the National Institute on Drug Abuse issued a comprehensive literature review including both abstracts of important papers and an "Overview" by Robert C. Peterson.[6] The discussion below will draw on both accounts; their conclusions are broadly similar.

Physical Effects

Marijuana burns at a higher temperature than tobacco, marijuana smoke contains 50 percent more carcinogenic hydrocarbons than tobacco smoke, and marijuana smokers typically inhale the smoke more deeply and hold it in the lung longer than do cigarette smokers. Thus marijuana smoking is likely to have effects on the respiratory system comparable to those of cigarette smoking, and probably at an equivalency of more than one cigarette to one joint; a recent study suggests a ratio of four to one.[7]

This is the only significant and well-established physical risk of marijuana smoking in otherwise healthy subjects. If one joint does as much damage as four cigarettes, an eight-joint-per-day marijuana user is smoking the equivalent in lung insult of a pack and a half of cigarettes per day. If such heavy marijuana smoking continued to years rather than months, or if it were added to cigarette smoking, it would seem to pose significant risk. This is particularly so since the average very heavy marijuana user is younger than the average very heavy cigarette smoker, and thus has more reason to worry about long-latency health problems like lung cancer.

Using the 4:1 ratio, an annual consumption estimate of 12 billion joints per year (see chapter 3) would be equivalent to about 2.5 billion packs of cigarettes per year. Since Americans smoke about 30 billion packs of tobacco cigarettes per year,[8] marijuana smoking constitutes a noticeable, but quite secondary, contribution to the total burden placed by smoking on the American lung.[9] The tax and other changes required to produce a given level of lung protection by decreasing cigarette consumption are certainly easier to bring about than the enforcement increase required to achieve the same lung protection by decreasing marijuana use.

Evidence of important physiological effects other than lung

damage is less convincing. Studies show reductions in testosterone production in male marijuana users have not been demonstrated to have clinical significance. Animal studies suggest increased reproductive failure in females, but studies in humans showing similar effects have been complicated by the lack of controls on other risk factors. The same is true of studies implicating marijuana in symptoms resembling those of fetal alcohol syndrome (although the consensus is that pregnant women should abstain from marijuana). Nor have reports of mutagenicity been confirmed, though the issue remains open.

Animal studies suggest that marijuana may also damage the immune system; some human studies find diminished immune response, others do not. Epidemiological evidence is negative so far but inconclusive.

Marijuana speeds up the heart rate during use. This has not been shown to be unhealthy for users with normal circulatory systems, but may pose problems for those with circulatory disease, which will tend to become more common among marijuana users as the user population ages.

Mental Health

Marijuana use can cause immediate unpleasant psychological side effects, such as disorientation, anxiety, and confusion.[10]

Use is also correlated with a number of behavioral problems, but whether as cause, effect, or product of a common third factor is unclear. The studies offer some evidence that the causal link runs more strongly from psychological problems to marijuana use than the other way around, since the problems tend to predate drug use.[11]

Some clinical reports link marijuana with the onset of mental illness, but the question of the direction of causation again remains open and the frequent presence of other drugs makes the significance of these results very difficult to interpret.

Concern about long-term effects of marijuana use on brain structure and function was stimulated by a British study published under the title "Cerebral Atrophy in Young Cannabis Smokers."[12] That study suffered from grave methodological difficulties—the subjects had used a wide range of psychoactives in addition to marijuana and were all suffering from clinical neurological disorders—and later, more careful studies have not confirmed its results.[13]

There are clinical reports of EEG ("brain wave") changes due to marijuana use, but again the presence of other drugs complicates the observation. Experimentally, EEG changes have been demonstrated during marijuana use, but do not seem to persist after use ceases. Studies of chronic user groups have found no persistent EEG changes, but these studies have also been criticized on methodological grounds.

Behavior

At the time of use, marijuana causes measurable deterioration in the ability to concentrate, to process complex information, and to coordinate eye and hand. Some studies have shown these effects persisting for months after extended periods of very heavy marijuana use, but none have shown permanent loss of function.

Half of high school seniors discontinuing drug use report concern about "loss of energy or ambition." Whether this refers primarily to the amount of time spent under the influence or to a more diffuse effect on personality is unclear, nor do we know what unprompted responses would look like. The only population studies of the problem have been in nonindustrial populations overseas; in these studies, lack of motivation is not one of the reported effects. However, those results do not obviously apply to the American situation, where the requirements for sustained attention and complex information processing are likely to be higher. Some clinicians believe that there is a distinct "amotivational syndrome" as a consequence of marijuana use; others do not.[14]

It appears that no one has carefully studied erratic behavior caused by marijuana. Studies on intoxicated driving, which probably represents the most important as well as the most obvious example of the problem, are complicated by the fact that there is no cheap, nonintrusive bioassay technique for detecting impairment due to marijuana. (Urine testing measures use over the previous thirty days, not current intoxication.)

There is no doubt that marijuana impairs driving performance, and does so more than the average user is conscious of. The open question is how frequently marijuana users drive while intoxicated, and what contribution they make to accidents. One study of 100 drivers killed in single-vehicle crashes found that 62 had blood alcohol levels greater than .09 percent, including six who also tested positive for marijuana. Another three tested positive for marijuana only. This suggests that marijuana's contribution to the problem of intoxicated driving is modest, and that either marijuana users do not often drive while intoxicated or that driving while in that state is unlikely to lead to a one-car fatality.[15] (One hypothesis: marijuana-intoxicated drivers may tend to do their unsafe driving at lower average speeds than do those under the influence of alcohol, and thus be less likely to kill themselves and others.)

There are also no contemporary clinical studies of marijuana-induced aggression, probably because no one expected to find any.[16] Whether for pharmacological or social reasons, marijuana does not appear to be an aggression releaser; observers are unanimous that crowds of people using alcohol are more likely to break out in fights than crowds using marijuana.[17]

None of this gives much evidence about whether marijuana intoxication is likely to lead to less dramatic forms of acting out, but the drug does not seem to be strongly implicated in the kind of life-ruining failures of self-command sometimes associated with the use of alcohol. Moreover, it appears that marijuana is likely to cause few of the disastrous effects on bystanders—automobile fatalities and criminal victimizations—to which alcohol is often linked. A drug that suppresses aggression rather than releasing it may damage its users but is unlikely to damage many others.

OTHER EVIDENCE

Statistical Sources

The National Institute on Drug Abuse publishes two statistical series on the magnitude of the drug abuse problem. The first, the Drug Abuse Warning Network (DAWN),[18] reports on medical examiners' findings of drug-abuse-related deaths and on admissions to an incomplete sample of hospital emergency rooms for acute drug reactions.

Of the 4,138 persons (outside New York City) reported by medical examiners as having died as a result of drug taking in 1986, only twelve cases mentioned marijuana. (When more than one drug is involved in a DAWN reported case all drugs are taken as "mentioned"; there are a little more than twice as many total mentions as decedents.) Of these twelve, ten involved other drugs as well, such as alcohol, cocaine or phenylcyclidine (PCP, or "angel dust"). Only two deaths resulted from marijuana alone, and these were termed "drug related" rather than "drug induced."[19] No lethal dose of marijuana has been established for any species.

Of the 119,000 emergency room drug episodes reported in 1986, only 6,064 (5 percent) mentioned marijuana, with about 75 percent of the mentions involving use in combination with other drugs.[20] These numbers may be slightly inflated because DAWN numbers are based on user self-reports of the drug or drugs involved, so a person who has a bad experience with PCP-laced oregano believing it to be marijuana will be reported as a marijuana accident.

For such a widely used and widely abused drug, these are small numbers. One can very roughly estimate the nationwide incidence of emergency room mentions from the DAWN statistics by multiplying them by 3.5, thus getting approximately 21,000 accidents for 1986.[21] Taking our estimate of 12 billion joints per year (see chapter 3), the total of 21,000 emergency room visits represents a rate of one visit per 571,000 joints consumed. Using the estimated population of 20 million current users, the 21,000 accidents translate to one accident per 950 user-years. Going further, if we count only cases that involve marijuana exclusively (25 percent of total), and assume that 75 percent marijuana is smoked by persons using no other drug at the time (9.75 billion joints), the 5,250 yearly accidents represent a rate of one emergency room visit per 1.7 million joints smoked not-in-combination, and one accident per 2,860 user-years of exclusive marijuana smoking.

By comparison, the estimated 5.7 million users of cocaine accounted for 1,092 deaths (26 percent of the total) reported in DAWN in 1986.[22] The rate of accidents per user-year, 87,000 (using 3.5 times the accidents reported in DAWN as explained above) is one accident per sixty-five user-years, fourteen times that of marijuana. Hallucinogen use is even more risky with 27,000 accidents (again multiplied by 3.5) for 960,000 current users, a rate of one accident per thirty-five user-years, twenty-seven times that of marijuana. Two hundred forty-seven deaths were reported.[23] DAWN does not keep statistics on emergency room visits due to alcohol, but one can presume that the rate of accidents per user-year would be extremely high compared with marijuana.

The numbers derived above are by no means precise; the exact figures are unknown and perhaps unknowable. The figures are, however, very useful in showing the *relative* danger of marijuana when compared with other drugs such as cocaine or hallucinogens. The exact rate of accident per user-year is unimportant in this case; what is important is that the relative chance of having to go to an emergency room is more than an order of magnitude greater for cocaine and hallucinogens than for marijuana.

Negative Evidence

At any given time over the last two decades, millions of Americans have been smoking marijuana. If there were important medium-term effects of moderate levels of marijuana smoking, they ought to be apparent by now. The fact that no one has been able to measure marijuana-induced disease epidemiologically should allow one to estimate an upper bound for any such effect, but no such calculation has been published. The same applies to the generation of birth defects, since there is now a large population of current and former marijuana smokers in the prime child-producing years. Of course, the significance of these negative findings is somewhat limited by the facts that the average potency of marijuana consumed appears to have risen over time and that users are starting younger and smoking more. Still, the silence of the literature on these issues is striking.

On the other hand, effects with long latency periods (e.g., cancer) have not yet had a chance to show themselves in the American population. These probably represent the largest possible source of major health damage due to marijuana consumption.

Fears of long-latency-period effects are intensified by the fat solubility of THC, which causes it to enter and remain in the body's fatty tissues, including brain cells, for periods of many days.[24] No one has suggested or detected a clinically significant result of this fact, but some researchers find it profoundly worrying.

SOCIAL COSTS

User Characteristics and Degrees of Harm

The frequency and severity of the harm imposed by marijuana use (along with, of course, any offsetting benefits) and how it varies with overall levels of consumption ought to determine our willingness to pay for reductions in the total amount of marijuana consumed by the American population. But marijuana is not smoked by populations; it is smoked by individuals who vary in a number of ways. If we can identify the characteristics of individuals or situations which tend to multiply the frequency and gravity of harm, we may be able to better focus our efforts to reduce consumption.

One person's marijuana smoking may be more harmful than another's for any of five reasons:

1. *Incompetence*. Our social arrangements assume that most people, most of the time, are capable of choosing their own actions in accord with their own interests. The greater the degree to which any individual is incapable of such determinations, the greater the reason for concern with his drug use.

2. *Vulnerability*. Some users may be more vulnerable than others either to physical, psychological, motivational, or behavioral damage generally or the effects of marijuana specifically.

3. *Escalation.* For some users, marijuana use may lead to increasing (and increasingly harmful) use of marijuana or of other more dangerous drugs in the future.

4. *Misbehavior.* Harm done to others is more clearly the business of public authorities than harm to oneself. There should be a special premium on reducing marijuana smoking by users whose behavior while under the influence tends towards victimizing others or recklessly putting them at risk.

5. *Poverty and dependency.* Since poor people have less money and often fewer other resources than others, damage to the poor is disproportionately likely to create demands on public resources and agencies. Since the capacities of those agencies are limited and their performance imperfect, preventing harm to the poor—including self-inflicted harm—has a special significance.[25] The poor may also warrant special concern if poor users are more likely than other users to commit crimes or harm others while intoxicated, or to increase their own drug use.

Populations of Special Concern

Drug use by children can claim somewhat greater social concern, ceteris paribus, than drug use by others, on all of the stated criteria.

1. *Incompetence.* Minors are conventionally treated as less able to make sound decisions for themselves, and thus more subject to control of their behavior, than are adults.

2. *Vulnerability.* A variety of harmful substances in a variety of species appear to do greater damage to organisms still in the process of development than to mature organisms. If this is true of marijuana in humans, then the medical harm done by a given amount of marijuana to an adolescent will tend to be greater than the harm done by the same amount of marijuana to an adult. Also, consumption of marijuana, as of any intoxicant, may interfere with learning in school, in which the public is held to be deeply interested.

3. *Escalation.* The more marijuana a person uses in any one time period, the more likely he is to continue his marijuana use and to become a user of any other given drug in the future. The same is true for virtually all psychoactive drugs, licit or illicit; current use of any drug predicts (in a statistical sense) future use of the same

drug and future use of any other drug.[26] (Attempts to determine empirically how much of this is causally significant and how much it reflects common underlying factors have not been successful.)[27]

Therefore, marijuana use by a younger person ought to be, other things equal, of more concern than marijuana use by an older person, just because the younger person has more years ahead of him. This is particularly so since use of illicit drugs, with the apparent exception of cocaine, seems to peak in the early twenties and taper off gradually thereafter.[28] A fifteen-year-old has about three times as many prime drug-using years before him as a twenty-five-year-old.

4. *Misbehavior.* It is possible that youthful marijuana use is more likely to result in crimes and accidents than is adult use. Statistics on drunk driving suggest that intoxicated youngsters are more dangerous on the road than are older intoxicated people, or that youngsters are more likely, once under the influence, to drive than are their elders. (However, on the other hand, a noticeable fraction of youthful marijuana use occurs among persons too young to drive.)

5. *Poverty.* Minors are also overrepresented among the group of marijuana users for whom the price of the drug is a major budget item, simply because their incomes are lower; this may lead to juvenile theft and drug dealing committed in order to support continued drug use.

It seems clear that youthful marijuana use, like youthful experimentation with alcohol, tobacco, and sexual activity, ought to be a particular social concern.

Another group of users deserving special concern are the heavy daily users—the "marijuanaholics." A small fraction of total marijuana users consumes a large fraction of all the marijuana consumed. The three million users at the top of the marijuana-consumption distribution smoke, on average, five to ten joints per day apiece, enough to remain intoxicated for most of their waking hours (on this point, see chapter 3). At this level of use, there is some experimental evidence of lasting brain changes and clear evidence of lung damage (see above), as well as, of course, near-constant intoxication with a mind-distorting drug. With respect to those (apparently a very small fraction of the population of heaviest users) for whom marijuana use is a compulsive behavior, the argument for singling them out is even stronger.

SOURCES OF PUBLIC CONCERN ABOUT MARIJUANA USE

We have argued so far that marijuana users pose little threat to others, and that the damage they do to themselves—beyond the loss of productive time—is largely speculative and probably less than that associated with many other psychoactives. Why, if this is so, is there such widespread public pressure for marijuana enforcement?

Factual Inconsistencies

There is a range of learned opinion about the physical and psychological dangers associated with marijuana use. In the service of campaigns to discourage use of the drug, the most negative opinions are naturally given as much prominence as possible. The double role of the National Institute on Drug Abuse as a research agency and an operational agency responsible for drug abuse prevention may also lead to an imbalance in the publicity accorded different laboratory findings. "Chromosome damage," "amotivational syndrome," and "cerebral atrophy" sound very scientific and frightening, despite the lack of demonstrated clinical significance of the first and doubts about the very existence of the last two.

There may therefore be a tendency among those who read newspapers rather than learned periodicals to overestimate the damage associated with marijuana use. This tendency will be exacerbated when there is a predisposition on nonmedical grounds to find the drug dangerous.

The Cultural Significance of Marijuana Use

Marijuana is a symbol of youthful rebellion, and its use by minors is a defiance of parental and legal authority. Whether there is a causal link—that is, whether reducing marijuana consumption would reduce the overall extent to which rebelliousness is felt and acted on—is unclear. However, this point may be lost on parents and teachers who encounter, or fear, both the drug and the other behaviors believed to be correlated with it.

Some of these actually or hypothetically correlated behaviors—dropping out of school, underachieving academically, using other more dangerous drugs, violating other laws—do demonstrable harm. Others—unconventional styles of dress and grooming; listening to rock music; increased sexual activity and enjoyment; interest in unconventional religions, arcane "sciences," and unusual diets; and scoffing at established authorities and institutions—are less demonstrably harmful, without necessarily seeming less threatening to parents. Even marijuana's suppression of aggression may make its use, particularly by male adolescents, appear to threaten cultural norms.

The Subjective Experience of Marijuana Use

It is widely agreed that the subjective experience of marijuana intoxication is more complex and subtle than the intoxication associated with alcohol. However, the nature of that experience remains poorly defined, at least in part because it is "... extremely variable and unpredictable—from one occasion to the next ... and from one person to another."[29]

Among the commonly reported effects are time distortion, enhanced emotional response to tastes, odors, sights, sounds, and textures, introspection and subjective dissociation, and feelings of great insight and creativity, often belied by review of the products in the cold gray light of dawn.[30]

All of this makes it understandable that parents of adolescents and others should regard marijuana use as a threat to cultural values important to them. It does not, however, provide a compelling reason for making the prevention of the spread of marijuana use an overriding policy goal, any more than the prevention of the spread of rock music, astrology, or macrobiotics.

The Insidious Nature of Marijuana Use

From the viewpoint of those who use it, marijuana has three great advantages: at low doses, the experience of intoxication can be quite mild and undramatic; most users never get beyond occasional use; and even quite heavy use has no immediately unpleasant aftereffects. This distinguishes marijuana from tobacco, most of whose users smoke at least several cigarettes a day and many of whom are addicted;[31] and from alcohol, whose "morning after" miseries are the stuff of folk humor and folk remedy.

Even the heavy, chronic marijuana user is likely to get few if any warning signs in the form of hangovers or other forms of physical suffering linked with drug use. A marijuana abuser's body, unlike an alcohol abuser's, is unlikely to complain very much: a sore throat is about the extent of discomfort he is likely to encounter.

From the viewpoint of those most worried about the spread of marijuana use and abuse, these advantages are traps for the unwary. If, in fact, low-dosage marijuana use is quite harmful, then users as a class would be better off if it gave them hallucinations and hangovers. If marijuana use is a threat to important shared values, then society might be better off if the drug's initial and obvious effects were more dramatic.[32]

NOTES

1. William Pollin, "Drug Abuse, U.S.A.: How Serious? How Soluble?" *Issues in Science and Technology* 3 (Winter 1987): 25. See also Mark Kleiman, letter to the editor, 3 (Spring 1987): 9–10.

2. William Novak, *High Culture* (New York: Alfred A. Knopf, 1980), includes a wealth of user reports of marijuana experience, most but not all from a favorable perspective. A discussion of insight and creativity occurs at pp. 122–133. See also Michael Kinsley, "Glass Houses and Getting Stoned," *Time*, 6 June 1988, 92.

3. See Thomas C. Schelling, "The Intimate Contest For Self-Command," *The Public Interest* 60 (Summer 1980): 94–118. Reprinted in Schelling, *Choice and Consequence* (Cambridge, Mass.: Harvard University Press, 1984), 57–82.

4. For some smokers, others will be concerned about their mari-

juana smoking when they themselves are not. This may be true for all the reasons that parents, for example, worry about activities of their children about which the children are unconcerned, or it may be a sign that the drug itself is causing changes in the accuracy of self-perception. For such measurable activities as driving a car, it is characteristic of marijuana smokers that they believe they are performing much better than is actually the case.

5. Institute of Medicine, *Marijuana and Health* (Washington: National Academy Press, 1982).

6. Meyer D. Glantz, ed., *Correlates and Consequences of Marijuana Use*, Research Issues no. 34 (Washington: Department of Health and Human Services, 1984).

7. Judy Foreman, "Marijuana Threat: New Research Finds the Smoke from One "Joint" Four Times that of Regular Cigarette," *Boston Globe*, 11 Feb. 1988, p. 1(A).

8. United States Department of Agriculture Economic Research Service, *Tobacco Situation and Outlook Report* (Washington: Department of Agriculture, September 1987), 5, gives an estimate of annual per capita adult cigarette consumption of 3,446 cigarettes per adult per year.

9. Marijuana's damage to the lung is subject to a technical "fix" not available in the case of tobacco: unlike nicotine, THC is not water-soluble. Thus marijuana can be smoked with various forms of water filtration, reducing "tars," particulates, and hot gasses while still delivering THC to the lung. This point would have greater practical significance if lung damage were the major source of social concern about marijuana use. The overwhelming bulk of current marijuana smoking involves joints, the form of smoking most dangerous to the lung; antiparaphernalia laws that restrict the availability of other equipment but leave rolling papers uncontrolled may contribute to this situation.

10. See Glantz, *Correlates and Consequences*, 5, 10, and the studies cited there.

11. Ibid., 4, and the studies cited here.

12. A. M. G. Cambell, M. Evans, and J. G. Thompson, "Cerebral Atrophy in Young Cannabis Smokers," *Lancet* 2 (1971): 1219–1225.

13. See the discussions in *Marijuana and Health*, 80–81, and Glantz, *Correlates and Consequences*, 10.

14. Mellinger et al. (abstracted in Glantz, *Correlates and Consequences*, 150–152), found marijuana use and academic achievement *positively* correlated among Berkeley undergraduates, perhaps due to the status of drug abstention as unconventional behavior at Berkeley

in the early 1970s. Michael Newcomb and Peter Bentler in *Consequences of Adolescent Drug Use* (Newbury Park, Cal.: Sage Publications, 1988), 147, found no link between marijuana use and poor school performance, but did find marijuana use connected to regressive coping behavior.

15. A. J. McBay and S. M. Owens, "Marijuana and Driving," in L. S. Harris, ed., *Problems of Drug Dependence, 1980* (Washington: Department of Health and Human Services, 1981), 257–263. Abstract in Glantz, *Correlates and Consequences*, 43–44.

16. See, for example, Gabriel Nahas, *Marijuana: Deceptive Weed* (New York: Raven Press, 1973), 44: "[M]arijuana use does not lead to violent crime. On the contrary, it inhibits the expression of aggressive impulses." Assertions, common in pre–World War II antimarijuana literature, of a link between marijuana and violent crime, are carefully demolished by John Kaplan in *Marijuana: The New Prohibition* (New York: The World Publishing Company, 1971), 88–140.

17. See Nahas, *Marijuana: Deceptive Weed*, 286.

18. National Institute on Drug Abuse, *Annual Data 1986: Data from the Drug Abuse Warning Network (DAWN)*, series 1, no. 6 (Washington: Department of Health and Human Services, 1987). Note that the medical examiner data excludes New York City.

19. DAWN, 54 and 190.

20. DAWN, 31 and 190.

21. This estimate is based on the percentage of the U.S. population living within the 27 major cities included in DAWN territory (29 percent) and the percentage of hospitals participating within these cities (76 percent), implying that only 22 percent of the accidents were reported. However, Judith Miller et al., in *National Survey on Drug Abuse: Main Findings 1982* (Washington: National Institute on Drug Abuse, 1983), 35–37, compared the populations of current marijuana users from metropolitan and nonmetropolitan areas. A reasonable estimate from these data is that there are 30 percent fewer current smokers in the nonmetropolitan areas. Multiplication by a factor of 3.5 is thus a reasonable, though certainly not exact, approximation of the nationwide accident rate.

22. National Institute on Drug Abuse, *National Household Survey on Drug Abuse: Population Estimates 1985* (Washington: National Department of Health and Human Services, 1987), 14, and DAWN, 54. This is using the rate of accident per user-year of use in combination as well as alone. Cocaine and hallucinogens are both mentioned as the sole drug 50 percent of the time (DAWN 116, 152), about twice as often as marijuana, so one can postulate that if the rate was cal-

culated using only exclusive use the difference between the accident
rates would be even more dramatic (such a calculation would need an
estimation of the percentage of time cocaine and hallucinogens are
used alone).

23. DAWN, 31 and 54, and *Household Survey*, 22.

24. *Marijuana and Health*, 22–23.

25. This point was brought home to me by Mark Moore's discussion
of the juvenile justice system.

26. See Kaplan, *Marijuana: The New Prohibition*, 203–206.

27. A brave try, using path analysis, is made in Richard R. Clayton
and Harwin L. Voss, *Young Men and Drugs in Manhattan: A Causal
Analysis*, Monograph no. 59 (Washington: Department of Health and
Human Services, 1981), 129–156. The issue of causation is discussed
in Kaplan, *Marijuana: The New Prohibition*, 205–212.

28. Judith Miller *et al.*, *Highlights from the National Survey on
Drug Abuse*, 198 (Washington: Department of Health and Human
Services, 1983), 12. See also Lloyd D. Johnston et al., *National Trends
in Drug Use and Related Factors Among American High School Stu-
dents and Young Adults*, DHHS Publication no. (ADM) 87–1535
(Washington: National Institute on Drug Abuse, 1987), 163–173.

29. Lester Grinspoon, *Marijuana Reconsidered* (Cambridge, Mass.:
Harvard University Press, 1971), 117.

30. See Novak, *High Culture*, 122–133. See also in Grinspoon, *Marijuana Reconsidered*, reviews of the nineteenth-century literary tra-
dition, clinical findings, and user reports (chapters 4, 5, 7, and 10).
Kaplan, *Marijuana: The New Prohibition*, reviews a number of casual
and scientific studies of users' subjective experience (pp. 70–94). Nahas, *Marijuana: Deceptive Weed*, reviews the same sources (except for
contemporary users' self-reports), and finds far more cause for concern
than do Novak, Grinspoon, and Kaplan.

31. Department of Health and Human Services, *The Health Consequences of Smoking: Nicotine Addiction*, prepublication edition
(Washington: Department of Health and Human Services, 1988), *i*.

32. Nahas makes this argument.

2

The Marijuana Market Problem and the Role of Enforcement

Virtually any prohibition creates a black market. In addition to reducing the effectiveness of the ban on consumption, black markets create social problems of their own beyond maintaining the supply of the drug to its users. Enforcement influences the size and shape of both the drug problem and the illicit-market problem, but in complicated and sometimes frustrating ways.

THE UNWANTED EFFECTS OF ENFORCEMENT ON ILLICIT MARKETS

Enforcement reduces the volume of marijuana sold and used. It seems logical that shrinking the market would concomitantly reduce its social side-costs. However, just as enforcement can sometimes exacerbate the drug abuse problem (for example, by encouraging undesirable substitutions), it can worsen the illicit-market situation as well.

Increasing Criminal Revenue

If marijuana demand is insensitive to price, enforcement will lead users to spend more on the drug because volume sold falls more slowly than unit price rises. This increased expense for users translates directly into increased revenue for sellers. Thus, enforcement can make the illicit market more lucrative and its participants wealthier. This extra revenue creates more numerous, richer criminals and allows suppliers to invest more heavily in resisting enforcement in order to maintain their business.

Enforcement Resistance

While increased enforcement may reduce the overall number of persons or organizations engaged in the marijuana trade, this reduction does not take place evenly across the spectrum of market participants. Being arrested is not entirely a matter of luck. While harming the average seller, heavy enforcement actually helps those individuals and groups who are the most skilled at evading enforcement through cunning, violence, and corruption. The removal of less skilled competitors improves the market share of the more skilled and ruthless.

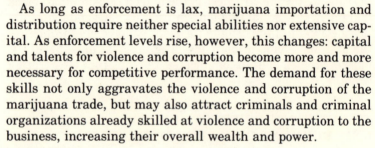

As long as enforcement is lax, marijuana importation and distribution require neither special abilities nor extensive capital. As enforcement levels rise, however, this changes: capital and talents for violence and corruption become more and more necessary for competitive performance. The demand for these skills not only aggravates the violence and corruption of the marijuana trade, but may also attract criminals and criminal organizations already skilled at violence and corruption to the business, increasing their overall wealth and power.

EFFECTS OF ENFORCEMENT ON CONSUMPTION

Marijuana enforcement is designed to reduce consumption. By adding to the costs of trafficking in marijuana, enforcement increases its price. Some users will continue to buy as much marijuana as before, but others will cut back on their consumption in the face of higher prices, or even stop smoking entirely. (A small number of dealers whose incomes rise with drug prices may actually increase their consumption, but this effect is likely to be negligible.)

An important set of questions without ready answers is how

Graph 2.1
The Size Distribution Curve for Marijuana Consumption

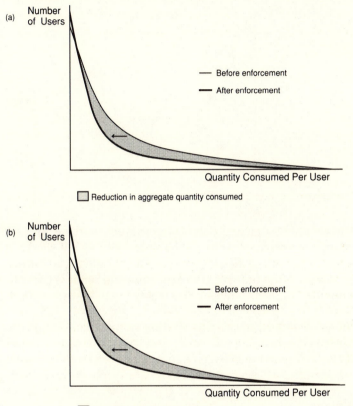

(a) Number of Users

— Before enforcement
— After enforcement

Quantity Consumed Per User

☐ Reduction in aggregate quantity consumed

(b) Number of Users

— Before enforcement
— After enforcement

Quantity Consumed Per User

☐ Reduction in aggregate quantity consumed

the reduction in marijuana consumption due to a price increase will be distributed among new and old users, adolescent and adult users, rich and poor users, and light and heavy users.

One way to describe the pattern of marijuana consumption at any given time is to plot the number of persons consuming various quantities of the drug. Graph 2.1 shows some of the shapes the size distribution curve for marijuana can take. The right-hand tail of the curve represents the behavior of heavy users.

Graph 2.2
The Demand Curve

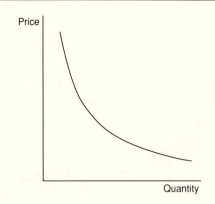

If most of the damage done by marijuana is done to very heavy users, a price increase will be most valuable if it shortens the right-hand tail of the curve, as shown in graph 2.1(a), rather than increases the number of nonsmokers and reduces the consumption of light and moderate smokers, as shown in graph 2.1(b).

The area under the size distribution curve equals total consumption. Its shrinkage as price rises gives the conventional negative relationship between quantity and price, the demand curve (graph 2.2). Even at the aggregate level, we know very little about the actual shape of the price-quantity curve for marijuana.

Reducing the amount smoked will tend to reduce the total harm done by marijuana consumption. However, enforcement can also exacerbate other kinds of harm. If enforcement makes marijuana smoking more costly, difficult, or dangerous than it used to be, fewer people will smoke it; but what they choose to do instead may be equally, if not more, harmful to themselves and to others than their marijuana use was in the first place. Those users who do not reduce their consumption will find that increased enforcement leaves them poorer, and perhaps worse off in other ways, than they were before.

Income Effects of Marijuana Enforcement

Neither the harm drugs do to their users nor the harm done by users to others is due solely to the effects of the drug. The money someone spends on drugs may be as important as the effects of drug consumption in causing suffering to the user and those in his social surroundings. This effect is observable at both ends of the income distribution: in the malnourished skid row heroin addict who acquires a criminal record because of the financial, rather than the physiological, aspects of heroin use; and in the high-income cocaine abuser who finds his punctured septum easier to repair than his shrunken bank account.

This generates a tension in making policy to control drug abuse. High prices discourage drug consumption; but, for a consumer of any given quantity of drugs, he and society will be better off the less he spends on those drugs.

How serious this tension becomes depends on how sharply the quantity consumed falls as the price rises or rises as it falls, that is, on what economists call the price-elasticity of demand. If the level of consumption of a given drug is responsive enough to price that higher prices reduce not merely the quantity that a given user consumes but the dollars spent (i.e., when the user's price-elasticity of demand is greater than unity), an increase in price will leave the user at a lower level of drug consumption and with more money left over for other expenditures.

Graph 2.3 shows that enforcement has a large effect on consumption when the demand curve is elastic; it also expands consumers' budgets. Consumer expenditure on marijuana before enforcement is the dark gray area; after enforcement, it is the light gray area. Note that the darker area is considerably larger than the lighter.

Assuming that, at the margin, the drug consumption in question is harmful, a higher price under these circumstances is better than a lower one from both a drug consumption perspective and a user-budget perspective.

But when the fall in drug consumption due to a higher price is less than proportionate to the price rise—as would probably be the case for marijuana—there will be a trade-off between reducing drug consumption and reducing drug expenditures as

Graph 2.3
The Effects of Enforcement on a Market with Elastic Demand

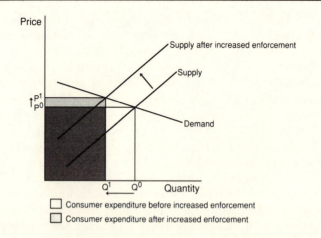

- ☐ Consumer expenditure before increased enforcement
- ☐ Consumer expenditure after increased enforcement

price varies. Higher prices will leave consumers less drugged-out but poorer. In this case, demand is inelastic, and enforcement has a minimal effect on the consumption of marijuana (graph 2.4). Moreover, it shrinks the consumers' budgets. Consumer expenditure on marijuana is the dark gray area before enforcement; after enforcement, it is the light gray area. In this case the lighter area is considerably larger than the darker area.

This trade-off will be of limited significance when drug expenditures are negligible fractions of users' budgets. One would have to be poor indeed for the five cents a tobacco cigarette costs to be among the best reasons for not smoking it. Since a moderately heavy marijuana habit can be maintained for a few dollars a day, expense is not a major problem for most marijuana users. The exceptions will be found among those with very low incomes (including some adolescents whose families are not poor) and those who smoke a great deal of marijuana.

Substitution

If enforcement makes marijuana use a less attractive activity, some consumers will look for substitute recreations. Some

Graph 2.4
The Effects of Enforcement on a Market with Inelastic Demand

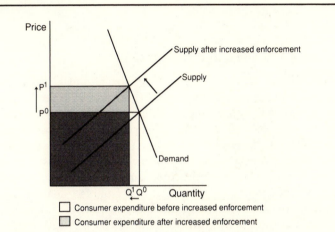

Price

P¹

P⁰

Supply after increased enforcement

Supply

Demand

Q¹ Q⁰   Quantity

☐ Consumer expenditure before increased enforcement
☐ Consumer expenditure after increased enforcement

of those recreations may be harmless; others, however, are considerably more harmful than marijuana. One likely harmful substitute is the use of other drugs, especially very inexpensive and very dangerous drugs such as inhalants and PCP (see chapter 6).

A more widespread instance of such substitution is the move towards consumption of domestic marijuana, which is significantly more potent than the imported product. The effects of greater potency in terms of qualitative and quantitative increases in medical risk remain unclear, but the fact that small amounts of marijuana now create a significantly higher level of intoxication in itself presents users with a sharper choice. Those who would often have chosen to get only slightly high must now choose between abstinence and a more profound intoxication. New users are now immediately initiated into the use of a much more potent drug, and heavy users are significantly more intoxicated (see chapter 10).

HARMS IMPOSED BY THE ILLICIT MARKET

The illicit marijuana market engenders violence and crime, participates in the corruption of public officials, demoralizes law enforcement and law-abiding citizens, contributes to the revenues of criminal organizations whose activities are not confined to handling marijuana, and complicates our relations with foreign governments.

Crime, Violence, and Corruption

Buyers and sellers of illicit drugs are potentially hostile to enforcement efforts, even beyond those directed at them personally or at the markets in which they are involved. In addition, some drug dealers use the criminal skills and working relationships developed in drug dealing to participate, as individuals and organizations, in other illicit enterprises. Unable to resolve their business disputes through legal channels or to appeal to the police against theft and violence, dealers in contraband are also both victims and perpetrators of violent crime.

Illicit markets generate opportunities for corruption, including systematic corruption, of law enforcement agencies. This criminality and its discovery undermine the legal system as a whole, well beyond the market involved or even illicit markets in general.

Fairness and Public Morale

Even without the direct contributions of black-market activities to other kinds of crime, illicit markets are demoralizing. Criminal wealth weakens both the perceived legitimacy and the incentive structure of the market economy. It moreover conveys a socially undesirable message about the relationship between respect for the law and personal well-being.

Perhaps more importantly, if either the illicit income-earning activity or the wealth of those who make their living at it are open and notorious, questions arise in the public mind about the competence and integrity of law enforcement. The belief that the only real crime is stealing small and getting caught is profoundly destructive to a culture of law-abidingness. This set of problems caused by illicit markets can be thought of as problems of perceived equity.

"Organized Crime"

All of the concerns and fears engendered by illicit drug markets generally, and by the marijuana market in particular, reach their pinnacle in the fear of "organized crime." Proponents of increasing enforcement levels sometimes argue that even if the consumption problem is minor or resistant to enforcement pressure, the burgeoning role of "organized crime" in marijuana dealing is reason enough for stepping up marijuana enforcement.

This claim might mean one of three things. It might suggest that the marijuana market is becoming a major revenue source for the established "families" of the Mafia or La Cosa Nostra, and is contributing to the special problems of violence, corruption, ill-gotten gains, and demoralization posed by these groups' criminal activities, both in illicit markets (for example, heroin importation) and in predatory crimes (for example, extortion).

The power that such "families" and their affiliates hold (or held until very recently) in political and trade union affairs makes them unique among criminal groups. If marijuana dealing indeed played a substantial role in keeping the Mafia in business, and if more enforcement could help put it out of business, marijuana enforcement could be justified on that basis alone.

Second, the claim might mean that groups now active in marijuana dealing threaten to develop the same characteristics of "organized crime" that now make La Cosa Nostra an especially troublesome organization.

Third, it could simply mean that marijuana dealing is perpetrated by criminal organizations which create violence, corruption, and wealthy criminals.

Using the phrase "organized crime"—long simply an ethnically neutral synonym for the Mafia—suggests the first concern. But, as we will see, La Cosa Nostra has virtually no role in marijuana dealing. The second concern is vastly implausible given the structure of the marijuana business; the third is simply a statement of the illicit market problem couched in inflammatory language. The dangers attributed to "organized crime" are the problems associated with illicit markets generally, rather than a special circumstance which could justify a policy of high enforcement levels. Moreover, increasing enforcement in a market like the marijuana market is more likely to increase rather than decrease the damage done by dealers, making them at once wealthier and more violent. (Organized crime is considered in more detail in chapter 8.)

Foreign Policy

American concern over marijuana and other drugs has led to demands for foreign cooperation and even threats of foreign sanctions over continued importation. Especially in periods when antidrug rhetoric is a staple of American politics, this can lead to compromising other American interests in drug-producing foreign countries. The political ramifications in the world arena of America's illicit drug problem are borne by all Americans equally, not restricted to consumers and sellers, or even to their neighbors, acquaintances, and communities.

Thus marijuana enforcement policy becomes a trade-off. Vigorous enforcement will reduce consumption, but it will also increase the importance of the most dangerous drug-dealing groups. Some users will benefit from reduced consumption, but the increased financial pressure and the substitution of more dangerous drugs will worsen the lot of others.

3

Marijuana Consumption Levels: 1986

INTRODUCTION: THE DEARTH OF EVIDENCE

How many people smoke marijuana? How much do they smoke? How much money do they spend? At least rough answers to these questions are essential to any serious analysis of enforcement choices. This chapter is an attempt to estimate the total annual consumption of marijuana in the United States and the total number of users, especially of heavy users, who constitute the drug's consumer population. The reader should be warned, however, that marijuana consumption and trafficking are wrapped in an obscurity so profound that expert opinions about both the quantity of marijuana consumed in the United States and its average retail unit price vary by more than 50 percent up or down.

Gathering information on these topics would seem to be a more-than-ordinarily worthwhile expenditure of resources for Justice Department investigators and prosecutors. However, the department has no budget for drug research, though its enforcement agencies learn something about the drug markets in the course of their investigations and are also privy to some information provided by intelligence agencies. Using this information allows some inferences to be drawn about both physical volume and dollar revenue in the illicit market drug markets.

The agency chiefly responsible for research on the drug problem is the National Institute on Drug Abuse (NIDA), a unit of the Alcohol, Drug Abuse, and Mental Health Administration in the Department of Health and Human Services. NIDA's medical perspective leads it away from doing the kinds of data gathering most relevant to enforcement planning: it does not tend to study either drug prices or the frequency and circumstances of drug purchases. NIDA does support two national surveys, one of whose results are used to estimate the size of the marijuana-consuming population.[1]

Trafficking-based estimates and NIDA's consumption-based estimates, though founded on different observations, are nevertheless estimates of the same quantities. Since all drugs imported or produced and not seized are eventually consumed (save whatever fraction is merely lost or rots in either dealers' or users' hands), the two methods of estimation should produce mutually consistent results. The job of reconciling them has been assigned to the National Narcotics Intelligence Consumers Committee (NNICC), an interagency group housed at DEA, whose annual *Narcotics Intelligence Estimate* is the official source for drug quantity figures. NNICC's task of reconciliation is not an easy one, either intellectually or bureaucratically. Until 1984, NNICC placed its primary reliance on trafficking-derived estimates. However, the consumer population estimated by NIDA could not plausibly have been consuming nearly as much marijuana as NNICC thought trafficking organizations were marketing.

CONSUMPTION-BASED ESTIMATES OF MARIJUANA CONSUMPTION

Survey Methods and Results

The primary source of information about consumption is the two NIDA surveys. These research two populations: persons twelve years or older living in households (for example, having fixed addresses—not transients—and outside such institutional settings as dormitories, barracks, and prisons) surveyed every two or three years by the Social Research Group at

George Washington University; and high school seniors sampled every year by a group at the Institute on Social Research of the University of Michigan.

As with any survey question about illegal or otherwise deviant activity, both underreporting because of fear or embarrassment and overreporting because of a desire to seem worldly-wise are potential problems. There is no easy way to guess how important these two effects are, which one is dominant, or how their relative importance varies across respondent groups. For example, it is a plausible speculation, but no more than a plausible speculation, that high school students might tend to boast about their drug experiences while older adults might tend to understate them. By the same token, changes over time may reflect changes in attitudes (which generate changing rates of over- or underreporting) as well as changes in actual behavior. Trend data thus need especially careful interpretation.

Perhaps surprisingly, a RAND Corporation review of studies that compared self-reports of illicit drug use with the results of urinalysis found overreporting to be as frequent and as large as underreporting.[2]

The surveys report on three categories of drug experience: "ever use," "current time," and "daily use."

Estimates of the first category are based on survey questions of the form "Have you ever used marijuana?" Projections of survey responses onto the national population arrive at a figure of between 50 and 70 million Americans who would, if asked, say that they had at some time used marijuana. That number is several times as high as it would have been twenty years ago, and it continues to grow, though not as rapidly. Since initiation into marijuana use is almost entirely restricted to the young, and since mass use of the drug is a post–1960 phenomenon, the number of Americans having ever used marijuana can be expected to grow well into the future, because while fewer than 5 percent of today's sixty-year-olds have tried the drug, more than 50 percent of today's thirty-year-olds (the sixty-year-olds of thirty years from now) have done so.

The "current use" category counts responses to the question, "Have you used marijuana within the last thirty days?" This

sort of question, in addition to deliberate under- and overreporting, runs into problems of "telescoping": a casual respondent's sense of time may be rather vague over periods of a
month. Respondents may inadvertently report behavior of six
weeks ago or omit behavior only three weeks old. In addition,
it may not be accurate to classify everyone who has used the
drug within the last thirty days as a "current user," since those
who have recently quit, those trying the drug once and deciding
not to continue, and those indulging in an annual fling will all
be included in the tally.[3] For some purposes a self-identification
question might be more valuable.

However, if the "current use" number is taken as an estimate
of the number of persons who have used the drug within the
past month, it is (allowing for under- and overreporting and
telescoping) a figure of interest. Its 1985 value is an estimated
18.2 million, up only slightly from the 1980 measurement but,
again, up vastly from twenty years ago. Of current users,
roughly 2.7 million are between twelve and seventeen years of
age, representing about 12 percent of that age group; 7.1 million are between eighteen and twenty-five, representing about
22 percent of that age group; 6.1 million are between twenty-
six and thirty-four, representing about 17 percent of that age
group; and the balance, some 2.3 million, are thirty-five or
older, representing about 2.2 percent of the final age group.[4]

"Daily use" is a term of art. The question asked of those
using marijuana in the previous month is "On how many of
the last thirty days did you use marijuana?" Anyone choosing
the category "twenty or more" is categorized as a daily user.
Clearly, this represents a measure of overstatement. In addition, there is evidence from commercial survey research that
this sort of question leads to systematic overreporting because
respondents have no precise sense of how often they carry out
a habitual activity. Questions like, "Did you use marijuana
yesterday? The day before? The day before that?" tend to lead
to lower estimates of activity. On the other hand, the restriction
of the survey to household residents probably understates the
size of this most deviant population, which likely includes
higher-than-average proportions of transients, inmates, and,
perhaps, dormitory residents.

With all these caveats, there seem to be roughly 4 million "daily" users of marijuana, approximately 22 percent of current users.[5] Of these, a little less than half can be assumed to use two joints or more a day.[6] This group, the "heavy daily users," would then number approximately 1.75 million.

Household surveys conducted before 1982 did not attempt to estimate either daily use or heavy daily use, so there is no way to guess population-wide trends. The high school survey reported a peak of 11 percent of high school seniors as daily users of marijuana in 1978, a peak from which the figure has fallen to 4 percent in 1986.[7] The 11 percent estimate caused great concern, as well it might, since daily marijuana use, even if it does nothing else, probably significantly interferes with studies, and since seniors, as nondropouts, were probably less at risk of very heavy drug use than eighteen-year-olds as a whole.

However, other data cast serious doubt on the validity of the 11 percent figure. The 1982 household survey estimates that only 4 percent of all young adults as current daily users. Furthermore, only 21 percent of the respondents aged eighteen to twenty-five reported themselves as *ever* having been daily users,[8] which implies together with the 11 percent estimate that, implausibly, over half of them were daily users specifically during their senior year of high school.

The household survey estimates, the only comprehensive survey source we have, give us the following sketch of American marijuana consumption in 1985, which both sample-selection bias and the results of the high school surveys warn us may be underestimates:

- Several tens of millions of Americans have tried marijuana, and this number will continue to grow for many years.

- Approximately 30 million Americans will use the drug in any given year, and about 20 million of those will use it in any given month. These numbers, having grown rapidly through the late 1970s, may now have reached a plateau or begun to decline.

- Approximately 4 million users smoke marijuana more or less every day.

- Approximately 1.75 million smoke marijuana twice or more per day.
- Total consumption of marijuana is 4,700 metric tons annually.[9]

Even though NIDA did not conduct a household survey for 1986, the estimates can be extrapolated from 1985 results. Total consumption was estimated by NIDA to have decreased only 4 percent from 1982–1985, and there is no reason to believe that there was a dramatic change in the rate of decline from 1985–1986.[10] Thus consumption for 1986 should be only slightly less than that for 1985, and for our purposes can be assumed to be the same.

Using the NNICC estimate that 18 percent of marijuana used in the United States in 1986 was domestic and assuming, rather arbitrarily, that a twentieth of imported marijuana and two-thirds of domestic marijuana is of connoisseur grade with a mean THC content of 8.4 percent,[11] then just under 16 percent of all marijuana consumed would be high-potency. This implies a total supply of 3,940 metric tons of low-potency and 760 metric tons of high-potency marijuana, and 850 tons domestic and 3,850 tons imported marijuana (see table 3.1).

One can look at this consumption estimate in terms of "joints" smoked. It has been estimated that an average joint of commercial-grade marijuana contains about four-tenths of a gram.[12] At 3 percent potency this represents some twelve milligrams of THC. This is conventionally supposed to keep one user intoxicated for about two hours. The estimate of 0.4 grams predates the dramatic potency increase of the last five or six years, and so may very well be an overestimate of the average size of a joint rolled today. Like the size of a joint, the term "intoxication" in this context carries considerable imprecision: there is no marijuana equivalent of blood alcohol content to serve as a standard measure of degrees of drug influence. Very new users, who have not "learned to get high," and very experienced users, who may have developed drug tolerance, may need to use more marijuana than occasional users to achieve the same subjective state. The 760 metric tons high-potency (the equivalent in THC content to 1,920 metric tons of low-potency) and the 3,940 metric tons of commercial marijuana would contain 195 metric tons of THC, and thus, assuming 20

Table 3.1
Marijuana Market in 1986

	Domestic (18% of market)	Imported (82% of market)	Total Market
Low Potency 3.33% $73/oz	281 tons 9 tons THC $727M	3,657 tons 122 tons THC $9.4B	3,943 tons 131 tons THC $10.1B
High Potency 8.43% $141/oz 16% of market	563 tons 47 tons THC $2.8B	192 tons 16 tons THC $953M	751 tons 63 tons THC $3.8B
Total 4.15%* $84/oz*	845 tons 56 tons THC $3.5B	3,850 tons 138 tons THC $10.4B	4,695 tons 195 tons THC $14B

*average for all marijuana

percent loss of the product due to consumer wastage and the presence of unsmokable material, would make up the equivalent of 12 billion standard (12 milligrams THC) joints, or between one and two joints per user per day.

Trafficking-based Estimate

The other approach to estimating marijuana volume is to start from drug seizure and enforcement data. Using this aproach the *Narcotics Intelligence Estimate 1985–1986* placed marijuana production and importation in 1986 at between 9,700 and 13,400 metric tons; after seizures and losses, NNICC estimates the net volume of marijuana available in that same year at between 6,700 and 9,400 metric tons.[13] This estimate places the percentage of marijuana lost to enforcement (and to poor distribution, spoilage, and other causes) at a high 33 percent; nevertheless the lower bound is still far above the consumption-based estimate. In what follows, we will use the consumption-based estimate for two reasons. First, it is more soundly based, while the trafficking-based estimates rely largely on untested rules of thumb. Second, for our purposes it is conservative; if the pessimistic argument of this book is persuasive assuming relatively low current consumption (for example, using the consumption-based estimates), it is persuasive a fortiori at any higher estimate. The larger the market, the harder it will be to influence, and thus the less difference any increment of federal resources will make.

Problems of Interpretation

Any discussion of marijuana consumption requires two caveats: one about potency, the other about tolerance.

Potency

Estimates both of marijuana production and consumption, usually given in gross weights, "joints," or frequencies-of-use, tend to treat cannabis as a homogeneous drug. Such figures ignore the important variations in drug potency across different marijuana types. A one-joint-per-week user may be actually inhaling more psychoactive substance than a four-joint-per-week user, and an apparent price increase and quantity decrease may really be a shift to more potent drugs that cost more per ounce.

Using the THC content of the drug as a proxy measure for marijuana potency only partially solves this problem. THC content varies by ancestry of the plant, its gender, growing conditions and treatment, the part of the plant from which the material is taken, and the age of the sample. The measured THC content of marijuana samples varies from below 1 percent to over 10 percent, with 3 percent being the norm for what users and dealers call "commercial" grades and anything over 5 percent qualifying as "connoisseur" product.[14] Under uncontrolled conditions, THC content decreases with a half-life measured in months.

Moreover, potency figures must also be interpreted carefully, since high- and low-potency marijuana are not perfect substitutes. Marijuana users report that the experience of smoking the one is qualitatively different from that of smoking the other, and that simple dosage adjustments to allow for THC content do not compensate for the difference. Weak marijuana is criticized as producing too much drowsiness and too little euphoria, while very potent marijuana is said to produce feelings of being "too stoned" or "out of control."[15]

Very potent marijuana may be connected with too-intense intoxication in any of three ways: the mix of psychoactive chemicals may be different; accurage dosage adjustments may be harder to make at higher concentrations of THC; and the strategy of "titration"—smoking until a desired level of intoxication is reached—may fail as the THC content per puff, and thus the THC consumed per unit time, rises. The pharmacological literature contains no reports of controlled experiments on different potencies of marijuana, although the clinical literature reports hashish as having somewhat different (and more profound) effects from those associated with even quite large doses of marijuana.

Large-scale importation and distribution, the primary foci of federal marijuana enforcement efforts, involve primarily lower-potency "commercial" grades of marijuana. Domestic growers, on the other hand, produce mostly a high-potency variety of marijuana called *sinsemilla* (Sp. "seedless"), cultivated by fairly sophisticated agronomy. NNICC estimated the 1986 market share of domestic marijuana at 18 percent, up from 15 percent in 1982.[16] Because of the ubiquity of domestic cultivation, estimates of domestic production are particularly unreliable (see chapter 5). However, if, very roughly, domestic marijuana consists of two-thirds high-potency marijuana averaging slightly less than three times normal potency, domestic marijuana would account for close to 30 percent—rather than 18 percent—of the effective volume of marijuana intoxication. This contribution would not be reflected in an analysis based on drug volumes or usage frequency.

Tolerance

The damage done by marijuana is determined by two quantities: the aggregate dosage, and the average amount of damage done by each dose. Total damage equals the product of these two factors; thus, if the amount used increases, we assume that the total damage done by the drug increases as well, and that the marijuana problem is getting worse.

Many calculations and arguments implicitly assume that the effect of each dose is constant. This assumption is especially important because, as we have seen, the wide variations in marijuana potency invalidate arguments based on the total weight of marijuana consumed. Arguments based instead on total THC consumption, person-hours of intoxication, or dollars spent (since the cost of a unit of THC is relatively constant) avoid this problem; but they are essentially dependent on the assumption of equivalent damage per dose THC.

The possibility that heavy marijuana users develop a tolerance for the drug complicates these calculations, since a given amount of THC consumed by heavy users would produce fewer person-hours of intoxication than if consumed by less experienced users. Insofar as intoxication is one element of the damage caused by the drug, tolerance implies that total damage is less than the product of the damage per use (for the median user) and the number of uses. The possibility that each joint has less effect as the number of joints any given user smokes increases means that higher dosages increase damage at a ratio of less than one to one.

Tolerance, then, should change the way we evaluate marijuana consumption. A consumption increase concentrated among high-volume tolerant users results in very little increase in the total number of person-hours intoxicated (although other effects, such as lung damage, may increase linearly or even faster). Similarly, any given consumption level may imply a smaller population of heavy users than calculations based on an assumed upper bound for an individual's consumption would indicate. In evaluating the amount of damage done by a given level of total consumption, tolerance makes the total amount smoked decrease in importance relative to the number of users above one or more cutoff points.

Although there is compelling evidence attesting to the existence of marijuana tolerance, clinical measurements are scant.[17] Until tolerance can be measured, consumption- and expenditure-based calculations continue to be the best methods available for determining order-of-magnitude estimates for marijuana use. Additionally, the population of *long-term* heavy users of marijuana appears to be quite small, decreasing the extent to which tolerance might confuse consumption-based estimates. Nevertheless, tolerance does seriously widen the margin of error for such calculations.

PRICE OF MARIJUANA

The conventional sales quantity for commercial-grade marijuana is the ounce (28 grams), with a retail price of approximately $70–75.[18] Assuming again 20 percent wastage, this will yield about fifty-six standard joints, at a unit price of about $1.30.

The total retail price of marijuana would come to about $14 billion using the prices of $73/oz. for commercial and $141/oz. for high-potency. The imported market would account for $10 billion and the domestic for $4 billion. Marijuana grown for personal use, given away by producers and dealers, or bought by users in quantities greater than an ounce would all reduce the actual total dollars spent on the drug.

The vast uncertainties in the numbers make trend estimation virtually meaningless, though NIDA does try, estimating a four percent decrease between 1982 and 1985. The following is the most that can be said with confidence: consumption, including very heavy consumption, grew rapidly from about 1963 to 1978; over the same period, attitudes toward marijuana use became more favorable. Subsequently, attitudes have reversed somewhat and the rate of spread of consumption has slowed; heavy consumption may have begun to decline.[19]

However, the measured ill effects of marijuana consumption (e.g., emergency room visits) still look very small compared to the quantity consumed (see chapter 1). Raising consumption estimates would only make the drug look even more benign. We have already estimated that 3 million Americans spend most of their waking lives "high" on marijuana. The fact that they don't seem to get into much visible trouble argues that the drug's ability to cause immediate harm cannot be very great. The number of hard-core alcoholics, persons who are drunk all the time, is nowhere near that large, and yet alcohol abusers show up in emergency rooms, treatment centers, and police stations in considerable numbers. The larger one imagines the number of heavy daily marijuana users to be, the more impressive (and reassuring) is their failure to come to the attention of the authorities.

NOTES

1. The first survey is National Institute on Drug Abuse, *National Household Survey on Drug Abuse: Main Findings 1985* (Washington: Department of Health and Human Services, DHHS Publication No. (ADM) 88–1586, 1988), with the related preliminary study, National Institute on Drug Abuse, *National Household Survey on Drug Abuse: Population Estimates 1985* (Washington, Department of Health and Human Services, DHHS Publication No. (ADM) 87–1539, 1987). These will be referred to hereinafter as the household survey. The second is L. D. Johnston, J. G. Bachman, and P. M. O'Malley, *National Trends in Drug Use and Related Factors Among American High School Students and Young Adults, 1975–1986* (Washington: Department of Health and Human Services, DHHS Publication No. (ADM) 87–1535, 1987). This will be referred to hereinafter as the high school survey.

2. K. H. Marquis et al., *Response Errors in Sensitive Topics Surveys: Executive Summary* (Santa Monica, Cal.: RAND Corporation, 1981), 4–5. Findings for other "sensitive topics," including alcohol use, were similar.

3. It is possible to make a rough estimate of the extent to which the household survey's current user figures are overestimates, by estimating the frequency of use among users who report use this year but not current use. If one assumes an average frequency of use among users who use less frequently than every month but at least once a year, one can calculate what portion of users reporting use in a given month are actually not current users but occasional users whose occasional use fell during the month preceding the survey.

Such an analysis is necessarily inexact, for a variety of reasons. The initial parameters are estimates; the analysis assumes no seasonal variation in use; and the model uses the figure for current use in two different capacities (to calculate the size of the yearly but not monthly user population and then as the sum of actual current users and occasional users using in the survey month). Nevertheless, the model can suggest the order of magnitude of the overestimates.

Such an analysis for 1985 shows that assuming that the average yearly, but not monthly, user uses only one month per year, the current user estimate of 18,190,000 current users overestimates by 930,000. A frequency of two months per year makes the current user figure 1,860,000 users too large; of four months per year, 3,720,000 users too large; of six months per year, 5,580,000 users too large; and of 10 months per year, 9,300,000 users too large.

4. National Institute of Drug Abuse, *National Household Survey on Drug Abuse: Population Estimates 1985*, 10.

5. See the household survey's *Main Findings*, p. 10 and *Population Estimates*, 41.

6. The 1985 household survey makes no estimates for heavy daily use. See the 1982 survey, Judith Miller et al., *The National Survey on Drug Abuse: Main Findings 1982* (Washington: Department of Health and Human Services, 1983), p. 6, and National Institute on Drug Abuse, *Highlights from the National Survey on Drug Abuse: 1982* (Washington: Department of Health and Human Services, 1983), 5.

7. Johnston, *National Trends in Drug Use, 1975–1986*, 50.

8. Miller, *Highlights*, 4.

9. NNICC, *Narcotics Intelligence Estimate 1985–1986* (Washington: Drug Enforcement Administration, 1987), 6. This is the "sanitized" (unclassified) version of the annual report of the NNICC, an interagency committee staffed by DEA employees.

10. NNICC, *Narcotics Intelligence Estimate 1985–1986*, 6, and Johnston, *National Trends in Drug Use 1975–1986*, 47–50.

11. NNICC, *Narcotics Intelligence Estimate 1987* (Washington: Drug Enforcement Administration, 1988) 9. NNICC estimates the potency of commercial-grade marijuana at 3.33 percent. NNICC bases its estimates on seizures, making the sample on which the estimate is based both small and unrepresentative. For the same reason, estimates fluctuate randomly from year to year, since one large individual seizure can skew the potency estimate dramatically. However, NNICC is the only available source and so must be used even with reservations.

12. Peter Reuter, "La Signification Economique des Marches Illegaux aux Etats-Unis: le Cas de Marijuana," in Edith Archambault and Xavier Greffe (eds), *Les Economies Non Officielles* (Paris: 1984), 92.

13. NNICC, *Narcotics Intelligence Estimate 1985–1986*, 15.

14. Hashish, which is the resin of the marijuana plant after it has been scraped off the leaves and flowering tops, has a THC content of approximately 20 percent, varying widely by variety. It is a somewhat special case, but for most purposes can be treated as a potent variety

of marijuana. The same is true of the misnamed "hashish oil," a concentrate of marijuana's active principles. Neither is now a significant item of commerce; NNICC estimates total 1983 hashish imports at 150 metric tons. *Narcotics Intelligence Estimate 1984* (Washington: Drug Enforcement Administration, 1985), 21.

15. William Novak, *High Culture* (New York: Alfred A. Knopf, 1980), 174–197.

16. NNICC, *Narcotics Intelligence Estimate 1984*, 16, and NNICC, *Narcotics Intelligence Estimate 1985–1986*, 15–16.

17. Meyer D. Glantz, *Correlates and Consequences of Marijuana Use* (Washington: Department of Health and Human Services, 1984), 5, notes some evidence of tolerance for psychological effects.

18. NNICC, *Narcotics Intelligence Estimate 1985–1986*, 8. Prices are given in broad ranges of which $73 is the geometric mean for commercial. *Sinsemilla* has a geometric mean of $141. The geometric mean (the number y between two numbers a and b such that there exists an x such that y equals the product ax equals the ratio b/x) is used because it is less sensitive than an arithmetic mean to the random fluctuations in the upper bound likely in these estimates.

19. Johnston, *National Trends in Drug Use 1975–1986*, 47–50.

SUMMARY: THE GOALS OF
MARIJUANA POLICY

What are the goals of marijuana policy? From the perspective of the marijuana abuse problem they are: reducing the total amount of marijuana consumed and its average potency; reducing use among minors, very heavy users, and the poor; and contributing as little as possible to users' health and financial problems. On the illicit market side, the goals are reducing the capacity of the market to supply the drug; limiting the violence and corruption occasioned by drug dealing; minimizing drug-dealing incomes; and limiting the flagrancy of both drug dealing and the disposition of its proceeds.

Policies which promote any number of these objectives may complicate or worsen others. The policies which most effectively reduce the capacity of the import industry will also often, though not always, work to the advantage of the groups with the guns, sophistication, and connections to resist the heightened enforcement. Increased pressure on domestic producers may encourage them to adopt dangerous "security" measures.

Successful enforcement against one supplier or group of suppliers will increase the power and income of the suppliers who remain. A low level of enforcement makes dealing marijuana easy, resulting in open and notorious but unpunished activity which demoralizes citizens and law enforcement officials alike. Increasing it can have the effect of replacing notorious but relatively peaceful marijuana sellers with more discreet and craftier sellers (who are also more likely to use violence and corruption in pursuing their trade).

Changes in the market will also result in consumer adaptations that might be either beneficial or detrimental to their health and well-being. Enforcement directed against imports may encourage the use of more potent domestic marijuana or of other drugs.

Most marijuana users pose little direct threat to others, and the medical and behavioral damage which the average user does to himself is still a matter for estimate rather than for measurement. Our central concern should thus be with classes of users for whom the damage done by the drug is disproportionately higher: the young, the poor, and the heaviest users, and with the illicit market whose corruption, crime, violence, and criminal income cause widespread damage.

The whole complex of marijuana "problems" creates a serious challenge for enforcement. The goals of policy are diverse and sometimes conflicting. Enforcement is a potentially valuable tool, but it may do harm in one area as it helps another. In Part II we will consider its potential and its costs.

Part 2

CHOOSING A MARIJUANA POLICY

It is 1982. You are an adviser to the new administration, which is pledged to do something about the drug problem. Your job is to figure out what can be done on the enforcement side to control the marijuana-consumption and marijuana-trafficking problems. Very substantial increases in resources are available if you think they will help.

You have already thought through the nature of the problems. What data do you need to gather and what analysis do you need to do in order to make a recommendation?

First, you need to understand how marijuana traffickers will react to a change, particularly an increase, in enforcement activity. This turns out to involve some complicated economic analysis, described in chapter 4, "Four Theories of Drug Enforcement Effectiveness." Given an abstract model of the relationship between enforcement and supply, you then need to plug in the current data on the dimensions of the marijuana markets and of the current enforcement efforts. Chapter 5,

"Supply and Enforcement: 1982," reviews the position as you face it.

Your next step is to try to calculate the effects of increased enforcement activity on the marijuana-consumption problem (chapter 6) and on the marijuana-trafficking problem (chapters 7 and 8). After examining some bureaucratic and organizational issues (chapter 9), you will be ready to decide whether pumping more resources into marijuana enforcement is likely to be a good idea. My idea about what your conclusion should have been is presented in the Summary of Part II, "A Marijuana Policy for 1982."

4

Four Theories of Drug Enforcement Effectiveness

Marijuana is a semiprocessed agricultural product. So is cured tobacco. But marijuana is much more expensive: a "joint" of commercial-grade marijuana has about $1.30 worth of marijuana in it, while a tobacco cigarette costs about a nickel. Marijuana is also somewhat harder to buy: its dealers don't advertise, rarely have fixed storefront locations, are at least slightly cautious about dealing with strangers, and are more likely to be out of stock on any given occasion than a convenience store is to be out of cigarettes. Moreover, the commodity sold as "an ounce of commercial Colombian" is likely to vary more in actual weight, potency, and the presence or absence of adulterants than is the commodity sold as "a carton of Winstons."

Part of the difference between the two markets flows directly from the simple fact that there are laws against selling marijuana, independent of the vigor with which those laws are enforced. Marijuana dealers' inability to advertise in the mass media or to enter into contracts that the courts will enforce (and thus, for example, to sell stock or borrow from banks) flows from the law and not its enforcement.[1]

But some of the differences between marijuana and tobacco arise from enforcement: the threat of imprisonment and confiscation of property (including and not limited to the marijuana itself) are part of the prevailing market costs. The greater the enforcement resources, the more costs can be imposed. In addition, being in prison, or even under indictment, limits the ability of individuals to buy and sell marijuana or otherwise carry on illegal dealings.

Thus the extent of enforcment influences both the cost structure of the industry and the number of participants in it. But how it does so is slightly mysterious. There appear to be three competing approaches to this question, based respectively on drug removals, on limiting the "through-put capacity" of the drug distribution system, and on price increases passed through to the consumer due to imposed costs.

None of these theories, however, can provide a complete explanation of the marijuana market's characteristics. We therefore propose a fourth, hybrid theory which starts with the cost imposition model but borrows some features from the through-put capacity model. That hybrid, the "learning curve" theory is more complex, not as easy to test against reality, and much less precise in the contingent predictions it makes about the results of enforcement changes than is the cost imposition theory. This chapter will discuss each theory and attempt to show why the cost imposition approach, despite its limitations, is the most useful of the four for the purposes of policy evaluation.

REMOVING DRUGS FROM COMMERCE

The simplest notion, which still occasionally appears in the rhetoric of enforcement agencies, is that enforcement does its work primarily by capturing drugs and "removing" them from supply. The implicit equation is, "production (or attempted import) minus removals equals consumption." The fallacy of this line of reasoning is almost self-evident: it assumes production (or attempted import) is determined independently of removals. But if the result of removals is unmet demand, what is to keep either current dealers or new entrants into the market from satisfying that unmet demand by bringing more drugs to market?

The drug removal theory would make sense only if the supply curve for the marijuana market was vertical or close to vertical (see graph 4.1). This would mean that the capacity of the world

Graph 4.1
The Drug Removal Model of Marijuana Enforcement

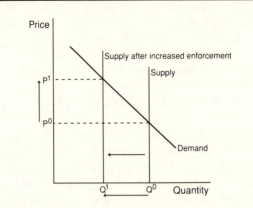

to produce marijuana (or at least to produce marijuana acceptable to consumers at something like the current prices) was somehow fundamentally limited.

But this is manifestly not the case, as the frequent swings in country-of-origin estimates for imported marijuana[2] and the very low prices of marijuana in source-country fields make clear.[3] If marijuana cultivation were difficult, the industry would not be able to spring up in various countries so quickly, and marijuana would be expensive rather than cheap at the site of cultivation.

Thus, if increasing enforcement decreases marijuana consumption, the drug removal theory does not explain why.

REDUCING THE THROUGH-PUT CAPACITY OF THE SUPPLY SYSTEM

Even if physical marijuana cannot be in long-term short supply, there might still be limits on the ability of marijuana dealers to acquire it where it is grown, arrange and finance its shipment to the United States, and distribute it to the final consumer down a chain of middlemen, none of them able to be sued and any of them capable of betraying his supplier to the authorities.

The difficulty and risk of finding trustworthy transaction partners in an illicit business might act both as a "barrier to entry" (keeping new marijuana-dealing firms out of the market) and as a constraint on the growth of existing firms. If this were the case, breaking up existing patterns of dealing among those who have learned to trust one another might reduce the overall through-put capacity of the marijuana supply system.[4]

Enforcement can disrupt such patterns and retard the development of new ones in three ways:

- by putting important participants in prison, thus preventing them from dealing during their stay behind bars;

- by causing participants to distrust each other either in particular (an individual under intensive investigation or indictment has strong incentives to betray his colleagues in hope of leniency) or in general (the more undercover agents there are pretending to be drug dealers, the riskier it is to buy from or sell to a purported dealer);

- by confiscating the drugs and money which are the "working capital" of ongoing drug-dealing organizations: if the existence of such an organization is what creates trust, and if the organization can be put out of business by the loss of working capital, taking assets may effectively destroy trust.

The through-put capacity theory implies that at any particular moment the supply of marijuana is limited, and increased enforcement reduces this supply. Enforcement can thus restrict supply and raise prices if it can succeed in disabling one or more large supply organizations.

This account is internally coherent, but theory and evidence suggest that it is unlikely to capture most of the truth about the marijuana market:

- The fluid nature of the imported marijuana industry (see chapter 5) suggests that "capacity" is likely to be an imprecise concept. As long as there are people waiting around ready to do another deal, there is untapped capacity. If existing capacity is not being used, then it must be final demand that limits the flow of drugs. In that case, it is hard to see how reducing through-put capacity (unless by a very large amount) would have any effect.

- Fluidity also suggests that breaking up organizations may not be a meaningful activity, since the trust relationships are individual-to-individual rather than organizational in nature.
- If through-put could not easily adapt to changes in enforcement or demand, then a string of enforcement successes in one area should leave a local supply shortfall. Consumers would either face sharply increased prices (as dealers ration limited supplies by price) or be unable to buy at all (if dealers use nonprice rationing). Yet enforcement estimates of marijuana prices, and of their regional distribution, are rather stable over time,[5] and high school seniors asked about the availability of the drug consistently report being able to find it.[6]

Thus the hope that increasing marijuana enforcement could limit marijuana consumption by restricting the ability of dealers to deliver the drug to customers seems forlorn.

COMPARATIVE STATICS: THE RISKS AND PRICES APPROACH

If neither marijuana nor the will to buy and sell it are scarce, then the quantity of marijuana smoked will be determined the same way the quantity of tobacco smoked is determined: by the costs of bringing it to market and the willingness of consumers to pay. If there are no barriers to entry, the long-run equilibrium price will, on average, just cover the long-term opportunity costs of the resources used in the marijuana business; if there were pure profits to be made (returns greater than could be earned by using the same resources elsewhere), existing firms would try to expand or new firms would enter the market and compete those unearned profits away.

By the same token, long-run profits will never be less than zero or resources would flow out of the industry; in the long run and on average, all costs will be passed through to consumers. Since at higher marijuana prices consumers will be expected to buy less marijuana, anything that raises costs will tend to depress the quantity consumed.

Many of the costs which drug suppliers face are imposed on them by enforcement. Lost drugs must be replaced. Employees facing higher risks of going to prison must be paid more, or

Choosing a Marijuana Policy

Graph 4.2
The "Risks and Prices" Model: Effects of Increased
Enforcement

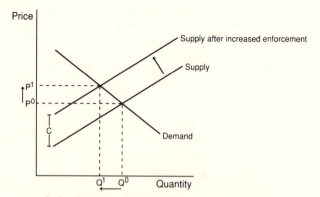

C: Cost imposed on dealers by additional enforcement

some of them will quit. Entrepreneurs, too, will want to make incomes high enough to compensate them for their chances of ending up behind bars. The absence of long-run pure profits implies that a small increase in risk, unless compensated for by a corresponding increase in expected income, will drive some marginal entrepreneurs into another line of business (or, perhaps more plausibly, fail to lure in new entrepreneurs as old ones quit). Changes in dealing patterns to avoid enforcement will also add to costs. The higher the level of enforcement, the more substantial these costs will be.

By this account, drug enforcement imposes a kind of "tax" on drug dealing. The drug "tax" decreases drug consumption just as the tax on spirits decreases alcohol consumption. More vigorous enforcement acts like a tax increase; it shifts the supply curve up, decreasing the quantity and increasing the price of marijuana (graph 4.2). Relaxed enforcement lowers imposed costs and functions like a tax decrease. It shifts the supply curve down, increasing the quantity and decreasing price (graph 4.3). This approach allows rather straightforward calculations of the likely effectiveness of enforcement in suppress-

Graph 4.3
The "Risks and Prices" Model: Effects of Relaxed
Enforcement

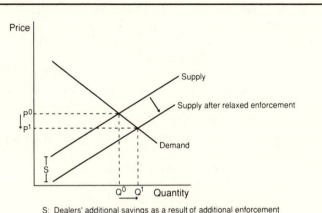

S: Dealers' additional savings as a result of additional enforcement

ing drug consumption. By summing the costs imposed by
enforcement on drug dealers and dividing that sum by the total
value of the market, one can calculate the "tax rate" that enforcement imposes on the target drug: if enforcement imposes
$950 million a year in costs on $10.4 billion market (for imported marijuana only), the "tax rate" is 9 percent. A program
of enforcement increases adequate to double all enforcement
outputs—drugs seized, assets seized, years in prison—should
roughly double the effective "tax," and thus increase the wholesale price of the drug by about 10 percent. (Increases in wholesale price will increase the capital costs of dealers at all levels,
so a 9 percent increase at wholesale might generate a 10 percent increase at retail.) Market shrinkage due to higher prices
and the costs of avoiding or confronting rather than suffering
it will boost this figure slightly.[7] A price increase estimate plus
an estimate of the price-elasticity of demand (a measure of
consumer responsiveness to price change) yields an estimate
of the effect of enforcement on consumption.[8] (See chapter 6 for
a discussion of the price-elasticity of demand for marijuana.)

Learning Curve Theory

Despite its superiority to the other theories we have discussed, the risks and prices approach, like the others, cannot explain one central fact. The price of marijuana seems to be far higher than the risks of the trade can explain: someone seems to be making considerable pure profit.

To make sense of this phenomenon, start with the simple observation that people who know what they're doing are more efficient in almost any activity than those who are still learning. Add the fact that, under drug market conditions, dealing with strangers is very dangerous, because there is no real substitute for experience in judging the honesty and reliability (as criminals) of one's transaction partners.[9]

If A sells B a ton of marijuana for the first time, A is somewhat uncertain about whether B will pay (rather than producing a gun) and B is rather uncertain about whether A will show up with the marijuana. Each faces the risk that the other is either a DEA agent or a genuine trafficker trying to "work off" a previous arrest by serving as an informant.

The second time the same two people engage in the same transaction, each has a much better idea about how the other will behave, and thus faces substantially smaller subjective risks. Organizations whose members have worked with each other before are thus low-cost producers compared with new organizations.

Dividing the market into "experienced" (low-cost) and "inexperienced" (high-cost) sectors is of course a simplification; the actual market involves a continuum. Any time an organization tries to grow substantially, it must take some risks, risks that may threaten its entire existing base. Thus an organization will be low-cost only up to some capacity limit; if it tries to do more, its marginal costs will be very high.

Consider then the entire collection of low-cost producers. Each one will have a capacity limit beyond which it loses some or all of its cost advantage. We will call the sum of those capacities the "low-cost supply."

On the other hand, there are potential entrants into the market who are not low-cost suppliers. At some price, it will

Graph 4.4
The Learning-Curve Model of the Marijuana Market

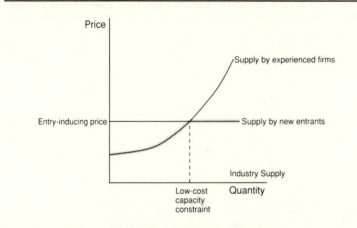

be just worthwhile for some of them to enter the trade. This point, at which new entrants have zero pure profits, is called in oligopoly theory the "entry-inducing price."

The supply curve for the entire industry consists of a mixture of the low-cost supply schedule and the new entrants' supply schedule (graph 4.4). Which of these schedules determines quantity supplied depends on the quantity demanded at the entry-inducing price.

If the quantity demanded is above the low-cost supply (graph 4.5), experienced firms will not fill the demand and room will be left for new entrants (who will thus accumulate experience and lower their costs in future transactions). Marijuana will trade at the entry-inducing price, and experienced dealers will reap quasi-rents on their low-cost position.

If, on the other hand, low-cost supply is greater than the quantity demanded at the entry-inducing price (graph 4.6), then there will be no room in the market for new entrants, and the price will be determined by competition among low-cost firms. Profits for low-cost firms will be reduced. In the extreme, if the entire market is served by firms with equally low costs, there will be no pure profits at all, and the price will be the competitive price despite the barriers to entry.

Graph 4.5
Learning-Curve Theory: Quantity Demanded at the Entry-Inducing Price is Greater than Supply by Experienced Firms

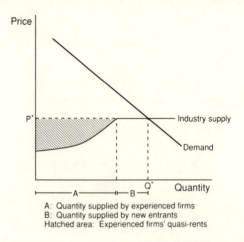

A: Quantity supplied by experienced firms
B: Quantity supplied by new entrants
Hatched area: Experienced firms' quasi-rents

If this theory is a good description of the marijuana market, what are its implications about the effects of enforcement?

Enforcement Against New Entrants

If the current price is at or above the entry-inducing price, increased enforcement aimed at new entrants will raise that price. (If not, there will be no new entrants to enforce against.) This will decrease consumption (with the decrease coming from the share of the new entrants) and raise the revenues and profits of experienced dealers, who will receive higher prices without incurring greater expense (graph 4.7).

Enforcement against Experienced Organizations

If the current price of marijuana is below the entry-inducing price, enforcement against low-cost suppliers is directed against the entire market. In this case, increased enforcement behaves as it does in the "Risks and Prices" model: it decreases quantity supplied, increases price, and has an indeterminate effect on suppliers' total revenue, depending on the elasticity of demand (see graph 4.8 a).

Graph 4.6
Learning-Curve Theory: Supply by Experienced Firms at the Entry-Inducing Price is Greater than Quantity Demanded

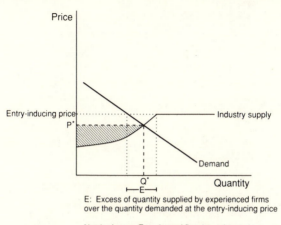

E: Excess of quantity supplied by experienced firms over the quantity demanded at the entry-inducing price

Hatched area: Experienced firms' quasi-rents

If, however, the total supply capacity of low-cost organizations does not satisfy demand at the entry-inducing price, the market consists of a mix of new and experienced firms. Increased enforcement aimed at low-cost suppliers has two effects. By increasing their costs of doing business, enforcement eats into their quasi-rents (since price is determined by the costs facing new firms only). Increased enforcement also destroys low-cost capacity through the incarceration of individuals and the disruption of trafficking patterns. Aside from increasing the market share of new entrants, this destruction has little immediate effect on supply conditions, since the entry-inducing price remains unchanged (see graph 4.8 b).

The Long Run

In the long run, low-cost capacity is not in fixed supply. It is continually created by the success of new entrants and the gradual growth of current low-cost suppliers, and continually destroyed by the retirement, incarceration, or death of market

Graph 4.7
Learning-Curve Theory: Enforcement Aimed at New Entrants

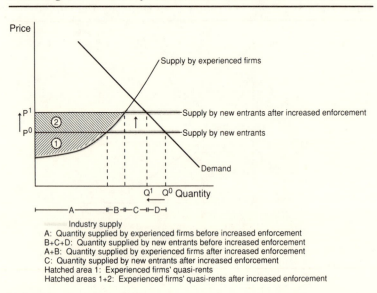

Industry supply
A: Quantity supplied by experienced firms before increased enforcement
B+C+D: Quantity supplied by new entrants before increased enforcement
A+B: Quantity supplied by experienced firms after increased enforcement
C: Quantity supplied by new entrants after increased enforcement
Hatched area 1: Experienced firms' quasi-rents
Hatched areas 1+2: Experienced firms' quasi-rents after increased enforcement

participants and the disruption of organizations and trafficking patterns by enforcement.

If low-cost capacity grows faster than it is destroyed, eventually it will be able to satisfy demand at the entry-inducing price. Price will then fall as low-cost suppliers compete with each other, rather than sheltering under the price umbrella provided by high-cost competition. Quasi-rents will shrink or even disappear (graph 4.9). (A familiar example of this in licit trade is the collapse of hand calculator prices in the early 1970s as manufacturers rushed to cash in on the fad.) This phenomenon seems the most likely explanation for the spectacular decline of cocaine prices during the 1980s—about fourfold at the kilogram level and even more than that at retail—despite robust demand and greatly increased enforcement efforts.

Thus enforcement efforts against low-cost producers, while they eat into quasi-rents in the near term, are essential to the continued existence of those quasi-rents. Enforcement against experienced organizations does for drugs what OPEC

Graph 4.8
Learning-Curve Theory: Enforcement Aimed at Experienced Firms

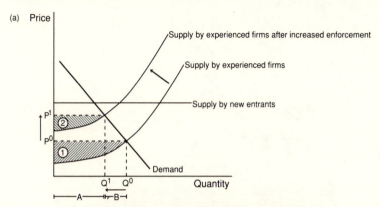

(a) Price

Supply by experienced firms after increased enforcement

Supply by experienced firms

Supply by new entrants

P^1

②

P^0

①

Demand

Q^1 Q^0 Quantity

A B

A+B: Quantity supplied by experienced firms before increased enforcement
A: Quantity supplied by experienced firms after increased enforcement
Hatched area 1: Experienced firms' quasi-rents before increased enforcement
Hatched area 2: Experienced firms' quasi-rents after increased enforcement

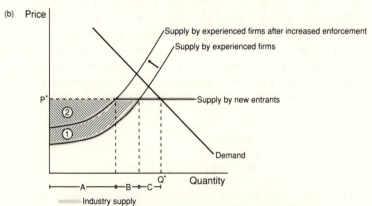

(b) Price

Supply by experienced firms after increased enforcement

Supply by experienced firms

Supply by new entrants

P^*

②

①

Demand

Q^* Quantity

A B C

Industry supply
A+B: Quantity supplied by experienced firms before increased enforcement
C: Quantity supplied by new entrants before increased enforcement
A: Quantity supplied by experienced firms after increased enforcement
B+C: Quantity supplied by new entrants after increased enforcement
Hatched areas 1+2: Experienced firms' quasi-rents
Hatched area 2: Experienced firms' quasi-rents after increased enforcement

Graph 4.9
Learning-Curve Theory: The Growth of Low-Cost Capacity

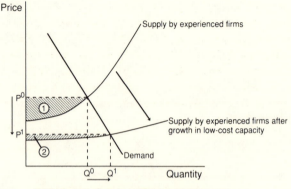

Hatched area 1: Experienced firms' quasi-rents
Hatched area 2: Experienced firms' quasi-rents after growth

(Organization of Petroleum Exporting Countries) did for oil: it limits the low-cost supply, thus maintaining supracompetitive prices.

All this leads to very confusing advice to policy makers. Enforcement directed at new organizations helps raise prices, but at the cost of boosting profits for experienced organizations. Enforcement directed at experienced organizations has no visible influence on the market, but unless low-cost capacity is continually removed, prices may collapse rather suddenly and quite unpredictably. The advocate of such enforcement is left in the position of the neurotic in the old joke:

Why are you snapping your fingers like that?
It keeps the elephants away.
But there are no elephants here.
Of course not. I've been snapping my fingers.

The problem with the learning curve theory as a tool for policy-making is that it requires more information than is ever likely to be available. In what follows, we will use instead the comparative statics, "Risks and Prices" approach. Aside from the goal of preventing a price collapse, this approach tends to be more optimistic about the value of enforcement than its more sophisticated alternative. Thus, if what follows establishes that marijuana enforcement is not a worthwhile activity under the "Risks and Prices" model, that conclusion will be true a fortiori if the learning curve model is correct.

This chapter has considered the theoretical capabilities of enforcement and their effects on supply. To know what effects enforcement actually will have on marijuana consumption requires knowledge about the shape of the demand curve and the amount to which enforcement is capable of shifting supply curves given the resources available to it. These are the topics of the next chapter.

NOTES

1. See Peter Reuter, *Disorganized Crime: The Economics of the Visible Hand* (Cambridge, Mass.: MIT Press, 1983), 109–131.

2. National Narcotics Intelligence Consumers Committee, *Narcotics Intelligence Estimate 1987* (Washington: Drug Enforcement Administration, 1988), 15–16; see figures for Colombian and Mexican market shares.

3. Peter Reuter and Mark Kleiman, "Risks and Prices," in vol. 7 of *Crime and Justice: An Annual Review of Research*, eds. M. Tonry and N. Morris (Chicago: University of Chicago Press, 1986), p. 293.

4. Mark Moore, "Limiting the Supply of Drugs to Illicit Markets," *Journal of Drug Issues* 9 (Spring 1979): 300–301. See also Moore, *Buy and Bust: The Effective Regulation of an Illicit Market in Heroin* (Lexington, Mass.: Lexington Books, 1977), 59–60, where this argument is made for heroin.

5. NNICC, *Narcotics Intelligence Estimate 1984*, 12, and the Domestic Unit of the Office of Intelligence in the DEA, telephone conversation 28 June 1988. Variations of price over region depend almost solely on the variations of transport cost from region to region and are relatively stable.

6. From 1975 to 1986 between 85 percent and 90 percent of high school survey respondents said marijuana would be "very easy" or "fairly easy" to obtain. L. D. Johnston et al., *National Trends in Drug Use and Related Factors Among American High School Students and Young Adults, 1975–1986* (Washington: National Institute on Drug Abuse, 1987), 152.

7. Reuter and Kleiman, "Risks and Prices," 305.

8. Cf. J. Michael Polich et al., *Strategies for Controlling Adolescent*

Drug Use (Santa Monica, Cal.: RAND Corporation, 1984) and Reuter and Kleiman, "Risks and Prices," 289–340, for similar calculations.

9. Some of the features of the application of learning curve theory to markets in illicit drugs are discussed in Peter Reuter, Gordon Crawford, and Jonathan Cave, *Sealing the Borders: The Effects of Increased Military Participation in Drug Interdiction* (Santa Monica, Cal.: RAND Corporation, January 1988), 109–121.

5

Supply and Enforcement: 1982

What are the mechanics of marijuana supply and enforcement? How are smuggling and domestic marijuana growing organized? How many smugglers and growers are there? How is the drug distributed? How much do marijuana traffickers earn? How are they organized? How successful are they? How much does federal enforcement cost? How much does it add to dealers' costs? The likely ramifications of changes in enforcement levels depend on the answers to such questions.

Unfortunately, our knowledge of the structure and function of the marijuana industry is inexact. The only hard information comes from investigative and trial records. These records do not represent a random sample of dealers, and the facts relevant to criminal guilt or innocence differ from those relevant to economic analysis. Case files and court transcripts are also of limited use.

The strategy of this chapter will be to try to construct a coherent picture of the marijuana market as it was in 1982. (For the balance of this chapter, except as noted, the present tense refers to 1982.) We will begin with the known facts and use economic reasoning and analogy with other illicit markets as methods. The chapter will describe the system in terms relevant to evaluation and try to get the gross magnitudes roughly right, rather than specifying details. The analysis in subsequent chapters is intended to be sufficiently robust to withstand significant changes in this description without falling apart.

(Changes since 1982 in the overall size and drug-by-drug composition of the federal drug enforcement effort may imply that the risks facing a marijuana dealer have grown substantially over the last few years. These changes are discussed in chapter 10.)

SUPPLY

Foreign Sources

Marijuana consumed in the United States in 1982 is largely (at least 85 percent) imported.[1] Since this figure represents gross weight rather than dollar value, and since American marijuana appears to be a disproportionately high-priced, high-potency product, the domestic product share of illicit revenues is higher, perhaps as much as a third of the total.

According to NNICC, an unreliable source but the only one available, two-thirds of imports came from Colombia; the remaining third came mostly from Jamaica and Mexico. These figures have been rather stable in the decade since Colombia replaced Mexico as the major source in the early 1970s as a result of the paraquat-spraying campaign that made Mexican marijuana virtually unsaleable in the U.S. market.[2]

The only major exception to the stability of market shares for source countries has been Jamaica, whose contribution seems to have fallen dramatically in the late 1970 for obscure reasons and recovered between 1979 and 1982 for reasons equally obscure.

The Mechanics of Importing

Almost all imported marijuana enters the United States by sea. "Mother ships"—ocean-going vessels—come north from Colombia and Jamaica with lots averaging about ten metric tons,[3] primarily to South Florida but also along the Gulf Coast and as far north as Maine. They are met at sea by smaller craft, capable of either running up on beaches or navigating inland waterways. The nature of these "offloading" vessels depends on the locale: shrimp boats in Florida and along the Gulf Coast, lobster boats off New England. (The exception to the mother ship/offloader pattern is smuggling across the Mexican border, where marijuana enters by truck or small plane, or in small quantities on the persons or in the vehicles of American or Mexican visitors. The small size of Mexico's 1982 market share and the paucity of data about the mechanics of smuggling from Mexico will lead us to neglect Mexican marijuana in the balance of this analysis.)

Marijuana usually changes ownership when it hits the beach. The load on the "mother ship" belongs to an "importer" (a conventional term among dealers and enforcement officials alike) who arranged for its shipment from the source country.[4] He will pay the exporter in the source country roughly $100 per kilogram.[5] The importer sells to a "distributor," who pays $250/kg and hopes to resell at $500/kg in ton lots.

The physical transfer from the mother ship to the landing site is handled by an "offloader." Offloaders, at least in South Florida, appear to be service providers rather than merchants. At no point in the transaction do they own the marijuana; they merely collect a fee for its safe transfer. This arrangement makes it possible to be an offloader without the risk capital required to buy and sell large quantities of marijuana, and therefore probably reduces the price of offloading services.

An enterprising DEA agent (named, improbably enough, Ted Weed) took advantage of the shortage of reliable offloading enterprises to mount what was arguably the most successful undercover operation in the history of narcotics enforcement: Operation Grouper.[6]

As a result of "Grouper," considerable knowledge is available about the South Florida marijuana import and distribution business in the late 1970s. There is no evidence that Grouper, fertile as it was of seizures and convictions, changed things substantially.

Weed and his colleagues established an offloading service that quickly earned a reputation both for reliability and for a remarkable degree of intuition about the activities of the Coast Guard. Not only did the service never miss a rendezvous, it never lost a load through seizure. Under these circumstances, no one appears to have noticed the extraordinary bad luck its customers suffered either at sea on the way to the transfer point or on the highways after the offloading was complete. For two years, until the operation culminated in mass arrests in 1981, the undercover offloading firm dominated the South Florida market, collecting video and audio tapes that helped produce a perfect record in the ensuing prosecutions: every defendant was convicted on every count.

The picture that emerges from "Grouper" is of a large group, certainly at least many hundreds, of marijuana entrepreneurs. In a given transaction, any one player might take on any of the three principal roles—importer, distributor, or broker between the two—or might play a subsidiary role as an employee of one of the principals or as a secondary distributor.

Some entrepreneurs had, or had access to, equipment and facilities (trucks and warehouses, for example). Others had regular employees. Rotation of roles depended in part on chance connections, in part on possession of capital; a dealer who had just lost a major load might be "tapped out," unable to finance a big transaction but willing to earn enough to get back into the game.

A group of people who deal with one another repeatedly learn about one another's habits: whose work is good, whose isn't. A reputation for reliability is a valuable business asset, one not to be lightly thrown away for short-term gains. This allows members of such a group to transact business with each other at lower cost than would be true of a group with less mutual knowledge about whom to trust and less to lose by cheating one another, particularly in a market where legal process for the enforcement of contracts is unavailable and betrayal the largest business risk. The existence of a business community within which participants have reputations to maintain is an asset to the entire group;[7] Peter Reuter has called it "relational capital."

Midlevel Distribution

Little is known about the structure of marijuana transactions in the vast middle range between a ton and an ounce. There have been a few federal cases against major regional distribution organizations with stable networks of lower-level dealers, but the relationships between major distribution groups and their "wholesalers" remain matters of speculation. Wholesalers may be employees, salespeople working on commission, "franchisees" with geographic or sociological territories, or merely buyers known to be reliable. They may have exclusive relationships with higher-level distributors or may buy from whoever is currently offering the most attractive mix of price, quality, and delivery.

Whether a wholesaler has connections with more than one distributor is an important question, because it helps determine how easily he can find a new source if his current supplier runs out of stock or leaves the business. A related question is whether new wholesalers can rise from the ranks of retailers simply by buying larger quantities, or whether entry at the wholesale level is controlled from above.

However, since federal enforcement activity is now directed almost exclusively at the top of the trade, and since the sheer number of market participants suggests that this is a virtually inevitable strategy, the "wholesale" level of the marijuana trade is not likely to be significantly affected by current or future enforcement programs.

Domestic Production

A noticeable and growing fraction (estimated at 15 percent for 1982) of the U.S. marijuana market is supplied by domestic production. The domestic marijuana industry bears little resemblance to the marijuana importing trade. Two major differences stand out: the size of the average domestic enterprise and the average potency of domestic product.

Unlike the fluid but hierarchical importation business, the domestic growing industry is highly atomized. "Firms" in the business are also much smaller than those that traffic in imported marijuana. This appears to be a function of transaction sizes. While the natural transaction in the importation market is for an entire boatload of many tons, the natural transaction in the domestic production industry is for a grower's crop. One

thousand plants, representing perhaps one ton of saleable marijuana, is a very big plot for a single domestic grower to tend.[8]

Two major groups of domestic cultivators make up the market. Most growers are amateurs, growing small plots for their
own use or sale to friends. A minority of domestic growers—
perhaps about 20 percent—cultivate marijuana full-time, using
greenhouses, hydroponics, and other sophisticated techniques.
They each produce between ten and fifty pounds of saleable
marijuana annually—together producing roughly 80 percent
of the domestic marijuana on the market—and giving them
gross annual incomes of between $20,000 and $100,000.

There does not appear to be any economic incentive for the
creation of large middleman operations in this market, and
they do not seem to exist.[9] Consequently, there is no point in
the process at which any one entity owns huge stocks of domestic marijuana.

There are two possible explanations for the fact that domestic
growing operations have remained relatively small in scale,
even as the domestic industry as a whole has grown. First,
cultivating marijuana plants, particularly of high-potency *sinsemilla*, requires considerable hand labor and fairly sophisticated agronomy. Since suitable growing locations are not
scarce, there is no reason for anyone capable of tending the
plants to go to work for someone else instead of setting up on
his own. Second, the need to conceal crops in the field from
enforcement authorities and from potential thieves creates diseconomies of scale for large plots. It also, incidentally, creates
a high incidence of booby traps and violent encounters between
growers, enforcement officials, and bystanders (hikers, absen-
tee landowners, and the like).[10]

Official and unofficial sources agree that high-potency marijuana constitutes a far larger fraction of domestic production
than it does of imports, although realistic quantitative estimates are not available. About one-third of the cultivated
plants eradicated in 1984 were classified as *sinsemilla*,[11] but
sinsemilla plots are typically smaller and less likely to be spot-
ted. *Sinsemilla* plants themselves also yield more, as well as
more potent, marijuana than their less-cultivated relatives.
Consequently, the fraction of *sinsemilla* in total U.S. produc-

tion is probably around two-thirds by weight, and an even higher proportion by value.

This higher-potency domestic product is not a perfect substitute for the lower-potency imports, because of price and because its effects differ qualitatively as well as quantitatively. Still, the two products are substitutes for one another. Since the domestic product largely escapes federal enforcement attention,[12] it benefits from efforts that increase the price at its substitute. The result will be high prices for the domestic product, an increase in domestic market share, or a mix of the two depending on the elasticity of the domestic supply curve.

Additionally, the rate at which current domestic growers expand production or new growers enter the market as the price increases can affect these results. Federal marijuana enforcement thus acts as a protective tariff.

ENFORCEMENT

What do federal enforcement agencies spend, and what do they accomplish in their antimarijuana efforts? They spend dollars, work-hours, and prison cells. They produce arrests, convictions, prison terms, drug seizures, and asset seizures.

Federal agencies involved in marijuana enforcement include the Drug Enforcement Administration (Department of Justice), the Coast Guard (Department of Transportation), the Customs Service (Department of the Treasury), the Internal Revenue Service (also Treasury), the Federal Bureau of Investigation (Justice), the Bureau of Alcohol, Tobacco, and Firearms (Treasury), the Immigration and Naturalization Service (Justice), and even the Forest Service (Department of Agriculture). Under the 1980 amendments to the Posse Comitatus Act, the military, while still forbidden to make arrests or seizures in civilian cases, is permitted to provide reconaissance information to domestic law enforcement agencies.

In addition, marijuana cases generate work for prosecutors in the U.S. Attorneys' Offices and in the Criminal and the Tax Divisions of the Justice Department, for the courts, and eventually for the prisons.

This activity is not centrally budgeted.[13] Instead, drug en-

forcement resource allocation is left to the normal budgetary
processes of the agencies involved. Furthermore, agencies involved in drug enforcement do not, in general, publish figures
to show which particular drugs were the subject of their activities. Even the DEA, which breaks down its activities by drug,
does not allocate its budget by drug. None of the other agencies
engaged in drug enforcement even breaks down activity by
drug, instead treating all drug enforcement as one budget line.
Total drug budget figures are also open to question in cases
like that of the Coast Guard, where units serve multiple functions—drug enforcement, prevention of alien smuggling, and
search-and-rescue—simultaneously.

The lack of accurage budget data is a problem both for analysis and for management; it is difficult to know how much the
U.S. government spends on marijuana enforcement, and it is
difficult for any one official to increase or decrease that amount.

In this instance, outputs are easier to count and measure
than are inputs. There is no ambiguity about whether a drug
seizure consists of marijuana or cocaine. Arrests and convictions also come with convenient drug labels, and from those
figures it is possible to estimate prison time as well.

Resources and Activities

Totals

The total 1982 drug law enforcement budget was $1.1 billion,
from a total federal drug abuse control budget of $1.4 billion.[14]
Of this, $862 million, or about 60 percent, went for interdiction,
investigations, internment, and intelligence, divided mostly
between the Drug Enforcement Administration, the Customs
Service, and the Coast Guard.[15] Of the balance, $116 million
went to the prison system, $39 million to prosecution, and $53
million to support overseas drug control activities of the State
Department (not all of which are enforcement).[16]

Allocation by Drug

Analysis of the allocation of the total drug enforcement
budget among drugs suffers not only from the scarcity of data

but also from two more fundamental problems. Drug enforcement has important elements of joint production both across drug classes and between drug enforcement and other agency missions (e.g., search-and-rescue for the Coast Guard). In addition, the marginal costs of some enforcement activities are well below their average costs. (Once the Air Force owns AWACS aircraft and has a trained crew, an extra hour in the air—even ignoring the training and readiness benefits—has fairly modest costs.) As a result, the figures below may overestimate the dollars that could be saved by cutting back marijuana enforcement. For resources within the Department of Justice, on the other hand, neither joint production nor fixed cost is a major factor: agent and prosecutor time and prison cells are reasonably linear in cost and can be used for only one activity at a time.

DEA agents reported spending 16 percent of their investigative work-hours in 1982 on marijuana cases.[17] Allocating the DEA budget of $243 million on this basis, the DEA marijuana budget was $39 million.[18] No such allocation is available for the FBI, but the main vehicle for FBI involvement in drug investigations is the Organized Crime/Drug Enforcement Task Force (OCDE-TF) program. While the OCDE-TF does not allocate resources by drug, it began in 1983 to publish a table of "drugs involved" in its cases. That year, of 851 total drugs in 467 cases, marijuana accounted for 222, or 26 percent.[19] Assuming that FBI agents working drug cases had previously allocated their efforts among drugs proportionately to OCDE-TF drug mentions, the FBI marijuana budget would be $10 million.[20]

Although there are figures for the drug budgets for both the Coast Guard and the Customs Service, neither of the two allocate its drug enforcement spending by drug class, and any allocation has a large element of arbitrariness due to "joint product" problems: a Coast Guard cutter may not know whether the vessel it is chasing carries marijuana, cocaine, or methaqualone until the search is made, and a large fraction of its time is spent in watching and waiting. For the Customs Service one can somewhat arbitrarily estimate that 30 percent of the budget is devoted to marijuana, giving an estimated drug budget of $56 million. One way to roughly approximate the marijuana drug budget is to use the percentage of drug arrests made which concern marijuana. For the Coast Guard this percentage is very high; in 1982, 98 percent of the drug arrests were for marijuana. Thus the estimated Coast Guard marijuana drug budget is $323 million. The Coast Guard spends more time on marijuana than the Customs Service because most marijuana moves by sea and by the boatload, while the Customs Service spends much of its effort investigating aircraft smuggling and searching passenger baggage and cargo for concealed drugs, including cocaine, heroin, and the "dangerous drugs."[21]

Although criminal cases differ enormously in the prosecutorial resources they consume, it seems reasonable to allocate drug prosecution costs across drug classes based on the number of cases brought. Since marijuana accounted for 25.8 percent of all DEA convictions in FY (fiscal year) 1982, we estimate the federal marijuana prosecution budget at roughly $10 million.[22]

Estimating prison costs is more complex. One way to look at the prison costs of drug enforcement is to examine current outlays: the Bureau of Prisons budget times the fraction of all federal prisoners convicted of drug offenses. This is analogous to using the current-year payouts of a pension system to calculate pension costs.

The alternative is to estimate how many years of prison time will be required to serve all the sentences imposed this year, allowing for early release in all its forms. This is analogous to the liability-accrual approach to pension costs.

The dramatic upsurge in drug enforcement over the last few years makes the second of the two calculations come out larger. Estimating according to current outlays, the National Drug Enforcement Policy Board puts total federal drug-related correction costs at $117 million in 1982.[23] Of this, approximately 25 percent represents marijuana cases, for a current-outlay budget for marijuana imprisonment of $30 million.

However, the long interval between arrest and disposition means that the imprisonment cost of the 1982 level of arrests was paid for up to two years later. In 1984 federal marijuana drug law violators were accruing effective prison time at a rate of 4,237 prison-years per year, almost 2.5 times the 1982 rate of 1,805.[24] This puts a considerable strain on a federal prison system that housed 30,000 inmates in 1985 in space with a rated capacity for 24,000.[25]

Since normal calculations of annual prison costs exclude capital charges, and since the federal system currently has no slack capacity, current average cost is a poor guide to the true marginal cost of drug imprisonment. If it costs, on average, $14,000 in operating expense to house a federal prisoner for a year,[26] and a new prison bed costs $50,000 at a capital cost of 10 percent per year, then each additional person-year of imprisonment costs $19,000. The total marijuana imprisonment cost for 1982 would thus be $34 million, while in 1984 the cost would jump to $80 million.

However, the long lead times that characterize prison construction make these calculations somewhat beside the point in the short run. If the federal prison population exceeds the system's design capacity, the result is either prison crowding or the release of some prisoners before their sentences have expired. Under these circumstances, the opportunity cost of resources used to accommodate an additional prisoner-year of marijuana enforcement may be considerably greater than $19,000.

Ignoring any excess opportunity cost of prison space over the $19,000 cost estimate, the total federal marijuana budget for 1982 includes $379 million for investigation, $10 million for prosecution, and $34 million for incarceration, a total of $423 million, of which $253 million represents arbitrary allocation estimates for the Coast Guard and Customs. Marijuana thus represents 38 percent of the 1982 adjusted federal drug enforcement budget of $1.1 billion.

Outputs

Drug Seizures

Federal marijuana seizures totaled 3000 metric tons in 1982.[27] Of this, assume that 60 percent (1800 metric tons) is seized on the high seas, 25 percent (750 metric tons) on the beach, and 15 percent (450 metric tons) from lower-level dealers. The 1,800 metric tons of marijuana seized on the high seas should be valued at between $20/kilogram and $100/kilogram, depending on the details of risk-sharing arrangements between exporters and importers. At the higher number, they would add $180 million to the total costs of the trade; at the lower number, $36 million. We will use $60 per kilo, or $110 million per year.

The 750 metric tons seized after they have changed hands "on the beach" should be valued at the landed price of $250/kilogram, for a total of $187 million, and the 450 metric tons seized further down the chain are worth perhaps $500 on average per kilogram, for a total of $225 million. Thus the total cost imposition from drug seizures is about $525 million.

Seizures of Traffickers' Nondrug Assets

DEA seized nondrug marijuana-trafficking assets worth $103 million during FY 1982.[28] This figure includes seizures and fines resulting from actions by the court system, IRS, Customs, and others.

This is likely to be an overestimate of what the asset seizure program actually costs the traffickers or yields to the government. This discrepancy has several causes. Some seized assets are returned to their original owners by court order. In addition, the final proceeds of the forfeiture of non-cash assets is rarely as great as the initial estimate. Some items are over-valuated at the time of seizure; others depreciate significantly between seizure and forfeiture; and a significant number carry liens and other debts payable to third parties which are deducted from the government's eventual proceeds. These factors, as well as the costs of maintaining seized items, suggest that the $103 million figure be treated as an upper-bound estimate.

Arrests and Convictions

Estimating the costs imposed on the trade by the risk of imprisonment involves a variety of problems. First, little is known about the mechanisms by which drug dealers learn about the risks they face. The most direct approach is to ask how much entrepreneurs and employees at various levels would need to be compensated to undergo small statistical changes in imprisonment risk, as workers in hazardous occupations are compensated for their risks by higher-than-normal wages. Econometric studies indicate that the risk of an additional accidental death in blue-collar trades adds between one million and five million dollars to total wages in that trade.[29] That is, if there were two otherwise identical jobs, each with 10,000 workers, but Job A had one fatality per year and Job B two fatalities, annual earnings per worker in Job B would, on average, be about $100 to $500 higher than earnings in Job A. Valuing a year in prison at $50,000 in increased wages is thus likely to be a reasonable estimate of the true impact of increased risk on the market, unless the sort of people who choose careers as drug dealers either put very high values on their lives or rate a year in a federal prison worse than a one-in-fifty chance of accidental death.

The top-level drug dealers, given their very high incomes, are likely to put higher values (measured in their own dollars) on their freedom than ordinary individuals.[30] How much higher is impossible to say, but we will calculate on the basis of $250,000 per year (five times as high as the value we have assigned to lower-level dealers).

The DEA system for evaluation of individual targets and prospective cases considers the drug involved, the monthly handling capacity of the organization under investigation, and the organizational role of the targeted individual. The system, called G-DEP, rates cases and individuals from Class I (highest) to Class IV, with a case taking the ranking of its highest ranked target. Class I and Class II cases are considered most important, and the fraction of any activity devoted to Class I and II cases or violators is a figure-of-merit in the DEA management system. Since DEA agents and supervisors have strong incentives to upgrade the cases they work on, any ranking above Class III is reviewed centrally. The review system and the incentives to upgrade create a situation where there are usually more Class III cases than Class IV cases, and almost always more Class I cases than Class II cases.

DEA calculates some statistics by drug and class; for example, one can find a figure for Class II cocaine cases or Class III dangerous drug cases. Other statistics are offered only by class. In what follows, it will be assumed that marijuana cases of any given class will resemble average cases of that class, unless separate data for marijuana are available.

In FY 1982, DEA made 3,301 marijuana arrests. Most of the lower-ranking violators were secondary targets in bigger investigations; almost half of all arrests occurred in Class I investigations.[31] DEA reports that there were 979 marijuana convictions in fiscal year 1982.[32] This does not imply a conviction rate based on the 3,301 arrests, because of the lags in case processing. The subsequent institution of a new case-tracking system at DEA caused an upward "bump" in conviction estimates of about 40 percent. This suggests that about 1,350 actual marijuana convictions grew out of DEA cases in 1982.[33]

Sentences and Time Actually Served

DEA provides data on average nominal sentence lengths (among those given prison terms at all) by violator class, and also gives the total number of sentences by violator class (table 5.1).[34] Dividing sentences by convictions gives the incarceration rate—the conditional probability of incarceration given conviction—for each class. A Bureau of Justice Statistics study found that marijuana defendants in general drew sentences similar to other drug defendants.[35] This provides some basis for the assumption that sentences for convicted marijuana dealers will resemble those of other drug dealers of the same class.

If that is the case, adjusting the DEA figures for sentence discount (the difference between nominal sentence and time actually served, due to statutory "good time" and parole releases), we can calculate the total annual effective time to be served by marijuana defendants due to convictions in FY 1982 to be 1,805 years (table 5.1). (Since DEA reports convictions in state as well as federal courts, some of this time will be served in state prisons.) That gives a cost impact of federal imprisonment of $250,000 per year times 424 years of imprisonment for Class I dealers, or $106 million, plus $50,000 per year times 1,381 years of imprisonment for lower-level dealers, or $69 million, for a total of $175 million.

Table 5.1
Federal Marijuana Offenders: Convictions, Sentence Lengths, and Effective Prison Time, by G-DEP Violator Class, 1982

Violator Class	I	II	III	IV	Total
Convicted	143	75	468	305	991
Sentenced to Prison (#)	130	62	391	163	746
Sentenced to Prison (%)	91	83	84	53	75
Average Nominal Sentence (months)	77	47	43	23	45
Average Effective Sentence (months)	28	20	20	17	21
Effective Sentence as Percentage of Nominal	36	42	47	76	46
Total Nominal (years)	834	243	1401	312	2798
Prison Time (% of Total)	30	9	50	11	---
Total Effective (years)	303	103	652	231	1289
Prison Time (% of Total)	24	8	51	18	---
Inflated Total (years) Effective Prison Time*	424	144	913	323	1805

*DEA disposition figures before 1983 are estimated to be 40% less than the actual figures.

Federal enforcement thus imposed costs totalling approximately $800 million on the imported marijuana market.

THE IMPACT OF ENFORCEMENT ON SUPPLY

Numers and Revenues of Drug Dealers

Estimating the numbers of participants at the top of the marijuana market poses great difficulties. Not only are the underlying numbers—number of consumers, quantity of marijuana, total revenues—subject to major uncertainties; not only are the models to convert these into a picture of the illicit industry highly speculative; but the fluid nature of the market means that stable roles may be as much the exception as the rule.

It appears that, at least in Florida in the late 1970s, many marijuana "firms" had a lifetime one transaction long, although the principals, employees, suppliers, and customers of those firms would appear and reappear, in various roles, in other transactions. In this context, the question "How many importing enterprises are there?" has no very well-defined answer: the number active on any given day will depend on the number of active transactions that day; the number active over the course of a year will be very large, far larger than the number of firms that would be required to handle the business if there were stable firms; on the other hand, the number active all year long will be very small.

Consequently, the analysis below will use the "deal," rather than the "firm," as its unit of analysis, and will analyze the risks and rewards of marijuana dealing on a deal-by-deal basis.[36]

Numbers of Dealers at Lower Levels

For importers at the top of the trade, the risks are moderately high, the rewards per transaction are great, and the transactions correspondingly infrequent. As the drugs move closer to the consumer, the risks and rewards per transaction are much smaller, and any one dealer will probably engage in a larger number of transactions per year.

The Customer-Ratio Calculation

The number of dealers depends on the number of customers with which each dealer is prepared to deal. The more customers, the higher the risk that one of them will be an agent or informant. On the other hand, dealing with more customers means making more money; a dealer has to balance risk and reward in making this choice. Marijuana is noticeably less risky than heroin in terms of both the risk of arrest and the risk of punishment given arrest.[37] If a heroin dealer is willing to deal with ten customers at a time, a marijuana dealer might handle four times as many.

For most consumers, marijuana purchases are infrequent events: a once-a-week smoker might buy an ounce each year. This distinguishes the marijuana market from, for example, the heroin market, where drugs are purchased daily for daily use. Thus a marijuana retailer can easily accommodate more customers than a heroin retailer, and in fact must do so in order to derive any substantial income from ounce-level transactions. It also suggests the futility of applying the retail crackdown strategy that has created some spectacular successes in the heroin market to the far more dispersed marijuana market.[38]

If there were 20 million marijuana users in 1982 and if each "retail" dealer supplies forty users, there would be some 500,000 persons regularly engaged in selling ounces of marijuana, each earning a little less than $5,000 a year; retail dealing is not a lucrative business. The kilogram dealers would make more money; around $25,000 a year. For the major players the risks and thus the benefits are much higher. Assuming 420 successful importations of 10 metric tons each, then the annual salary for an importer would be $150,000, while a major distributor would receive $125,000 (table 5.2).

Enforcement Risks at Lower Levels

Assuming five employees each for enterprises that buy metric tons and sell 50-kilo lots, and further assuming that kilo

Table 5.2
The Imported Marijuana Industry in 1982

	Number	Purchase Unit	Sales Unit	Purchase Price/kg	Sales Price/kg	Total Revenue	Value Added	Persons /Entity	Value Added /Entity
Users	20M	1 oz	---	$1600	---	---	---	---	---
Oz. Dealers[1]	500k	1 kg	1 oz	$1050	$1600	$6.7B	$2.3B	1	$4,600
Wholesalers[2]	50k	50 kg	1 kg	$750	$1050	$4.4B	$1.3B	1	$25,200
Middlemen[2]	5k	1 ton	50 kg	$500	$750	$3.2B	$1.1B	5(?)	$42,200
Distributors	420[3]	10 ton	1 ton	$250	$500	$2.1B	$1.1B[4]	20(?)	$125,000[4]
Importers	420[3]	10 ton	10 ton	$100	$250	$1.1B	$630M[4]	10(?)	$150,000[4]
Exporters	?	10 ton	10 ton	$20	$100	$500M	$440M	?	?
Collectors[2]	?	?	?	$5	$20	$110M	$82M	?	?
Farmers	?	---	?	---	$5	$28M	$28M	?	?

Assumed total quantity: 4,200 metric tons
Assumed average retail price: $45/oz

[1]Includes imputed profits of self-dealing; excludes sales of domestic product
[2]May represent multiple levels
[3]Successful transactions
[4]Per-transaction figures

sellers are sole proprietors, we estimate that there are 75,000 persons involved in the marijuana traffic between the distribution level and the retail level. These dealers share among them the risk of 1,050 years in federal prison, and thus average five days in federal prison (or in state prison for DEA cases) per year of activity. They also share an additional 1,000 years spent in state prisons and local jails.[39]

All of the above calculations are internally consistent and conflict with no known fact. They should not be treated as precise, however, due to the wide uncertainties involved (table 5.1).

SUMMARY: THE MARIJUANA MARKET

Imported marijuana has a complex distribution chain. The chain begins with importers who import the drug in shiploads of many tons and ends with retailers, who distribute it in ounce and kilogram lots. Value is added at every step; markup is between 40 percent and 200 percent at each of six or seven levels. Importation is mostly by sea onto the Florida coast, but marijuana is also smuggled across the rest of the eastern coastline and over the Mexican border.

Domestic marijuana, which accounts for slightly under 20 percent of the market, has a shorter distribution chain. Domestic cultivation, unlike importation, presents significant diseconomies of scale; it produces primarily a higher-potency, higher-priced product.

The federal government's drug enforcement budget for 1982 was approximately $1.1 billion. About 40 percent of the total, $423 million, was spent on marijuana-related investigations, prosecutions, and incarcerations. The government seized about 3,000 metric tons of marijuana and $103 million in nondrug marijuana-related assets that year, and kept about 1,800 drug dealers in prison.

This activity imposed costs of roughly $800 million on the imported marijuana industry, a figure equal to roughly 11 percent of its revenues. It did not significantly affect the industry's ability to deliver its illicit product to consumers.

NOTES

1. NNICC, *Narcotics Intelligence Estimate 1984* (Washington: Drug Enforcement Administration, 1985), 5.

2. This campaign is occasionally cited as an instance of successful crop eradication. However, contemporary DEA documents make clear that in the immediate aftermath of the first spraying Mexican marijuana was widely available at a discount to its Colombian substitute ($15/oz. v. $25/oz.) but found few takers, suggesting that paraquat destroyed the market rather than the crop. Recent (1984) huge seizures in Mexico may force a re-estimation of the Mexican share of American imports. Earlier estimates may have been at fault, or there may have been real change since 1982.

3. Thaddeus R. Mitchell and Robert F. Bell, *Drug Interdiction Operations by the Coast Guard: Summary* (Alexandria, Va.: Center for Naval Analysis, 1980), 15. The CNA estimate, prepared for the Coast Guard, is based on seizure statistics, probably as good as any. Ten metric tons is consistent with DEA agent beliefs.

4. Roger Warner, *The Invisible Hand: The Marijuana Business* (New York: Beech Tree Books, 1986), 40.

5. In at least some cases, according to DEA reports, the source county seller ("exporter") shares the risk of interception with the importer; payment of $20/kg is made on loading, with the remaining $80/kg due on successful landing.

6. Robert Pear, "155 Indicted as Two-Year Federal Drug Inquiry Ends," *New York Times*, 13 March 1981, p. 12(A).

7. Peter Reuter, *Disorganized Crime: The Economics of the Visible Hand* (Cambridge, Mass.: MIT Press, 1983), 152–53.

8. The roughly 20,000 plots eradicated by DEA-supported state and local marijuana eradication efforts contained a mean of 190 plants and a median of 128 plants. Drug Enforcement Administration, *1984 Domestic Cannabis Eeradication/Suppression Program Final Report* (Washington: Drug Enforcement Administration, 1984), 6–8. The 1984 National Drug Strategy document points out that the U.S. Attorney for the Eastern District of California personally prosecuted a case involving four growers and 4,400 plants, implying that such a case was deemed worthy of special attention. Drug Abuse Policy Office, *National Strategy for Prevention of Drug Abuse and Drug Trafficking* (Washington: National Drug Enforcement Policy Board, 1984), 56.

9. Warner, *The Invisible Hand*, describes an attempt to create a large organization to deal in domestic marijuana, and why it came apart. For income and volume estimates for domestic growers, see pp. 156–57.

10. Ibid., 204ff.

11. DEA, *1984 Domestic Cannabis Report*, 8.

12. "... the nature of domestic production places it primarily within the jurisdiction and capabilities of state and local authorities." *National Strategy*, 56. See also Warner, *The Invisible Hand*, 234.

13. Even when the 1984 crime bill gave the Attorney General the title of "Drug Czar" and formal authority over drug enforcement activities outside the Department of Justice, it did not create a unified drug budget.

14. Drug Policy Office, *National and International Drug Law Enforcement Strategy* (Washington: National Drug Enforcement Policy Board, 1987), 182–188. No separate allocation is made for the court system. This publication is hereafter referred to as *IDLES*.

15. Additional monies went to the FBI; IRS; Bureau of Alcohol, Tobacco, and Firearms; Forest Service; Marshals Service; and Immigration and Naturalization Service.

16. *IDLES* 1987, 182–186.

17. Hunter W. Peil, Chief, DEA Statistical Operations Unit, telephone conversation March 1988.

18. *IDLES* 1987, 182–186.

19. Organized Crime Drug Enforcement Task Force Program, *Organized Crime Drug Enforcement Task Force Program: Annual Report* (Washington: Department of Justice, March 1984), 80. This will be referred to hereafter as the "OCDE Task Force Report."

20. Based on FBI drug budget figures of $40.1 M (*IDLES* 1987, 182). This is a strong assumption, since the FBI drug budget authority more than doubled between 1982 and 1983. The total dollar figure is sufficiently small, however, not to significantly affect the analysis.

21. Based on 1982 drug budgets of $185.5M for Customs and $329.2M for the Coast Guard (*IDLES* 1987, 182–186). The Coast Guard made 1,088 arrests in 1982, 1,065 of which were for marijuana (From the data base of the office of Operational Law Enforcement, Coast Guard, August 10, 1988).

22. DEA Headquarters Statistical Services Section, personal communication, 22 March 1988.

23. *IDLES* 1987, 186, 188.

24. The 1982 figure is derived later in the chapter. The 1984 figures are from the DEA's *Annual Statistical Report 1984* (Washington: Drug Enforcement Administration, 1985).

25. "Department of Justice FY 1986 President's Budget Request," 4 February 1985 (DOJ handout to Congressional staff). Projections of future prison populations in this document do not seem to reflect the

calculation below of the massive demands current levels of drug enforcement activity will put on the prison system.

26. This estimate is obtained by dividing the federal prison population (28,133) into the Bureau of Prisons budget ($382M). (Bureau of Prisons, *Bureau of Prisons Annual Statistical Report Federal Year 1981–82* (Washington, Bureau of Prisons, 1982), 109, and U.S. Office of Management and Budget, *Budget of the United States Government Federal Year 1982* (Washington: U.S. Office of Management and Budget, 470.) The projected budget was $392M; the actual budget was even greater at $435M, thus making our figure a lower-bound estimate.

27. *Organized Crime Drug Enforcement Task Force Program: Annual Report*, table 9, p. 73.

28. NNICC, *Narcotics Intelligence Estimate 1982* (Washington: Drug Enforcement Administration, 1983), 69.

29. W. Kip Viscusi, *Risk by Choice* (Cambridge, Mass.: Harvard University Press, 1983), 99 and 101. See also Michael J. Moore and W. Kip Viscusi, "Doubling the Estimated Value of Life: Results Using New Occupational Fatality Data," *Journal of Policy Analysis and Management* 7 (Spring 1988): 476–490.

30. Although, as Peter Reuter has pointed out, the typical drug dealer is unusually willing to risk his freedom, his high income nevertheless makes him apt to value his freedom more highly than would other individuals. Two distinct factors contribute to this willingness. First of all, wealthy persons can afford to pay higher absolute sums to maintain their freedom than those with ordinary incomes. Second, the lucrative nature of the drug trade means that dealers forego substantial income while incarcerated; therefore, the opportunity cost of losing one's freedom is unusually high.

31. DEA, personal communication; 1,536 Class I cases divided by 3,325 cases total yields 46 percent.

32. DEA, personal communication.

33. Conviction figures for marijuana vary widely. OCDE-TF reports 1,538 convictions (and 3,683 arrests) in CY (calendar year) 1982 (see *Organized Crime Drug Enforcement Task Force Program: Annual Report*, 67–68). The office of the U.S. Courts reports 2,936 marijuana convictions for the period 1 July 1981 to 30 June 1982 (which includes non-DEA arrests). (See *Federal Offenders in U.S. District Courts 1982* (Washington: Administrative Office of the U.S. Courts, 1983), appendix table X–1, p. X–1–32).

34. DEA, personal communication.

35. Bureau of Justice Statistics, *Federal Drug Law Violators* (Washington: Department of Justice, 1984).

36. This strategy was suggested by Mark Moore.

37. Peter Reuter and Mark Kleiman, "Risks and Prices," in vol. 7 of *Crime and Justice: An Annual Review of Research*, ed. M. Tonry and N. Morris (Chicago: University of Chicago Press, 1986) discusses this issue in some detail.

38. For a discussion of the risks of heroin dealing, cf. John Kaplan, *The Hardest Drug: Heroin and Public Policy* (Chicago: University of Chicago Press, 1983), 99f.

39. See Polich et al., *Strategies for Controlling Adolescent Drug Use* (Santa Monica, Cal.: RAND Corporation, 1984), 58–63.

6

The Dynamics of Marijuana Demand: Enforcement Effects on Consumption

Federal enforcement can affect marijuana consumption in three ways: by raising prices, by creating shortages, and by changing the mix of products available on the market. From where our hypothetical decision maker stands in 1982, the important question is by how much—using any of these methods—increased marijuana enforcement could reduce marijuana consumption. That question is the topic of this chapter; the next chapter will consider the effects of increased enforcement on the drug-trafficking aspects of the marijuana problem.

CONSUMPTION DECREASE DUE TO PRICE INCREASE

Insofar as increased marijuana enforcement reduces consumption by increasing price, the size of that reduction depends on two factors: the magnitude of the price increase and the responsiveness of consumption to changes in price (for example, marijuana's price-elasticity of demand).

Price Increase as a Result of Increased Enforcement

Of the three theories of drug enforcement discussed in the previous chapters, only one—the "Risks and Prices" model—

generates a quantitative prediction of the price increase likely to follow from an enforcement increase. (The through-put-capacity model suggests that the major impact of enforcement is to create physical shortages; this prospect is discussed in the next section.)

The dynamic learning curve model, which reflects the complexity of the real world better than the comparative statics approach of "Risks and Prices," suggests that price will vary critically depending on the detailed nature of the trafficking industry and of the enforcement effort. On the one hand, the model suggests that some of the new costs imposed on the market by enforcement increases will be absorbed by the quasi-rents currently being earned by inframarginal, well-established dealing organizations rather than being borne by consumers as higher prices.[1] On the other hand, it suggests that prices for the whole market are set by the costs imposed on new entrants or rapidly growing firms; if enforcement is concentrated on them, prices might rise faster than indicated by the ratio of costs imposed by the new enforcement effort to total revenues.

Thus the relatively straightforward calculation of costs imposed suggested by the "Risks and Prices" theory may be only a rough approximation of the actual effect of increased enforcement on price. With that warning, and in the absence of the data needed to generate quantitative predictions from the learning curve model, we will proceed to make that calculation, using the 1982 estimates in chapter 5.

Federal enforcement imposed costs totalling approximately $800 million on the imported marijuana market in 1982. Total revenues in that market—the total retail price of *imported* marijuana—were about $7.2 billion. Enforcement-imposed costs thus constituted 11 percent of the retail price, 19 percent of the kilo level price and 39 percent of the price at the ton level.[2]

Now assume that doubling the enforcement effort will double all enforcement outputs: arrests, convictions, prison years, drug and asset seizures. That assumption seems wildly optimistic; it is about the same as assuming that twice as many fishermen on the same lake will catch twice as many fish.

These increased enforcement costs, and the secondary effects on capital costs in the industry, would generate about a 13 percent price increase at retail, a 21 percent rise in kilogram-level prices, and a 44 percent rise in ton-level prices.[3] This will underestimate the price impacts of enforcement increases to the extent that it ignores the costs of avoiding enforcement rather than suffering it. But it is hard to imagine these costs—extra labor time, equipment, and bribe money—running into the hundreds of millions. If much of the huge bill of a marijuana enterprise represents compensation for the risk of prison time, then the cost of an extra hour waiting for the coast to clear may be rather low.

The Price Elasticity of Marijuana Demand

Marijuana is inexpensive. Our earlier calculations suggested an average 1982 retail price of eighty cents per joint that might keep a user "high" for about two hours (see chapter 1). If eighty cents is taken as the price of this two hours' recreation, the recreation is cheap relative to users' budgets and alternative recreations. (If marijuana-induced craving for sweets ["the munchies"] leads the user to eat a bag of caramel corn, for example, the caramel corn will cost more than the marijuana.) Taking the eighty cents and the two hours as the combined cost of the drug experience, the two hours are the overwhelming consideration for any but the most impecunious user.

This suggests that marijuana demand is not likely to respond dramatically to small changes around its current price. Unfortunately, none of the available data about marijuana prices and quantities, and no available survey data, allow a direct numerical estimate. However, Eugene Lewitt and Douglas Coate have made a very careful study of the price-elasticity of demand for tobacco cigarettes.[4] They found an overall price-elasticity of demand of $-.42$—a 1 percent price increase would yield a quantity decrease of less than 1/2 of 1 percent.

Of the overall price-elasticity of $-.42$, only $-.10$ represents the decrease in cigarettes smoked per smoker, a very low elasticity estimate consistent with the habitual nature of tobacco smoking. The other $-.32$ reflects the effect of price change on the smoking participation rate. This makes intuitive sense: given that most smokers quickly progress to the one-to-two-pack-per-day level, where tobacco costs $300–$700 per year at current prices, the price of cigarettes ought to be a serious consideration for the potential smoker. Once started, however, tobacco smokers have difficulty cutting back on their use of the drug.

The considerations for marijuana are somewhat different. The weekly marijuana user spends only about $45 per year on the drug, and some additional money on rolling papers or pipes. Thus, the initial decision to take up the drug has far less serious financial implications than does the decision to take up tobacco. This suggests that the effect of price on the participation rate would be lower for marijuana than for tobacco.

On the other hand, very heavy marijuana users, the three million or so that we have estimated smoke an average of eight joints per day, spend about twice as much on marijuana as a two-pack-a-day smoker does on tobacco. Moreover, marijuana use appears to be less diffficult to give up or cut back than is tobacco use: while tobacco smokers (and heroin users) use a wide range of commercial products and services designed to help them quit, such services are still largely unknown in the marijuana market. These facts might suggest a higher price-elasticity among very heavy marijuana smokers than among heavy tobacco users.

There may also be a significant distinction between demand for physical marijuana and demand for marijuana intoxication. If, as prices rise, users can find ways to smoke more efficiently—to capture a higher fraction of THC in any given physical quantity of marijuana—then marijuana consumption might drop more quickly than does the total quantity of THC delivered to users' brains.[5] Most users presumably would prefer to improve their efficiency—even with some inconvenience—than to reduce their effective drug consumption, although such changes in habits seem to be more typical of "price shocks" produced by sudden dramatic changes in price than by the 10–20 percent variations in price at issue here. (Of course, such consumer economizing will not create benefits in terms of drug abuse, although it will reduce illicit-market revenues.)

Consumers might also begin smoking the more potent domestic marijuana as the difference between the price of the foreign and domestic varieties decreased. This might cause the price of the domestic marijuana to increase as it experienced less competition from the foreign product, resulting in an overall decrease in marijuana purchased. If however, the domestic market is capable of expanding at or near current unit costs, domestic production would grow, at or near current prices, to meet the increased demand, resulting in consumers' switching to the more potent domestic product rather than curtailing their marijuana habits.

A more significant long-run effect of a price increase might be to limit the extent to which marijuana is freely shared in social settings. If such sharing is an important mechanism in the initiation of new marijuana users, the consequent reduction in the initiation rate might be important.[6]

Even so, it seems unlikely that the impact of a moderate marijuana price increase on marijuana consumption through changes in the initiation rate will be anywhere near the $-.32$ Lewitt and Coate estimate for tobacco cigarettes, just because the financial implications of starting marijuana use are so much less serious.

This upper-bound estimate of the impact of price increases on existing users is extremely discouraging from the viewpoint of reducing marijuana abuse by increasing enforcement. The price-elasticity of marijuana demand among current heavy users would have to be a multiple of the Lewitt and Coate estimate of $-.10$ for tobacco to give a 20 percent price increase, much in the way of drug abuse control benefits. Moreover, given the components of the price-elasticity of demand for tobacco cigarettes, it seems likely that marijuana demand is less, rather than more, sensitive to price than that of tobacco.

If the price-elasticity of demand for marijuana were as great as a highly unlikely -0.4, then the 13 percent retail-level price increase which was our upper-bound estimate of the effect of doubling enforcement would yield a consumption decrease of imported marijuana of 5 percent, a meager result for so dramatic a budget reallocation.[7]

SHORTAGES

Creating Shortages

Marijuana grows virtually anywhere, and growing it requires no special skill (though growers' skill does contribute to potency). It can be grown in enormous plantations or small plots; though the field price of the drug is a small fraction of its price to the consumer, it is quite lucrative as raw agricultural products go. This leads farmers to overproduce compared to expected demand. A marginal acre whose product has only a 10 percent chance of being sold is still worth planting.[8] Large fractions of the crop therefore go unsold; the gap between estimates of production abroad for export to the United States and estimates of United States consumption reflect this situation.

For this reason, it is extremely unlikely that the physical supply of marijuana should ever be in worldwide shortage. The crops now grown but not harvested or sold, and the crops sold at low prices to consumers in producer countries, provide a "buffer" against shortages in the rich marijuana-importing countries. The very small share—less than 1 percent—of the final consumer price accounted for by the price at the farm gate indicates how insignificant raw materials acquisition is in the business of marijuana smuggling and illicit distribution. It also implies that very much more expensive growing methods than are now used could be resorted to, if market conditions warranted, without much effort on consumer prices.

The almost instantaneous growth of Colombian cultivation and smuggling in response to the destruction of the market for Mexican marijuana by paraquat spraying in the early 1970s support this line of reasoning.[9]

Moreover, marijuana importation requires not much more than a boat or airplane (perhaps rented or stolen) and a small amount of capital. Such low costs for market entry make the importation system as a whole, like production, unlikely to run out of physical through-put capacity.

Shortages of marijuana, when they occur, are thus phenomena of the distribution system. A local or regional wholesaling cartel linked to one or a few importing or distribution groups might find itself "dry" if all or most of its suppliers were put out of business. It might respond by imposing rationing rather than increasing price, either as a conscious strategy or for reasons linked to its organizational structure.

But it is hard to imagine how such shortages could become chronic. Neither supplier relationships nor conventional prices are absolute, though both may be sufficiently stable that a temporary crisis will not disrupt them. A local organization chronically unable to deliver market-clearing supplies would either attempt to raise prices or look for new sources not only in order to reap the financial rewards but to prevent an entry-inducing situation in its market. The more it appears that a shortage is chronic rather than temporary, the greater the rewards for new entrants challenging the local cartel's power. A few months—a growing season plus some start-up time—would seem to be the likely outer limit on the duration of a local or regional marijuana shortage.

As noted above, marijuana shortages seem to be rare. In 1982 88 percent of high school seniors report that they could easily obtain the drug if they wanted it.[10] The high school survey does not ask about earlier periods of unavailability, but region-to-region reports of current availability do not fluctuate from one biennial survey to the next as they would if there were occasional regional shortages.

Consumption Effects of Temporary Shortages

A heroin shortage has an almost instantaneous impact on heroin consumption. This is because heroin users buy a daily supply of heroin each day, partly because they lack adequate cash for bulk purchases, and partly because of an inability to hold personal inventory without consuming it all immediately.[11]

A marijuana shortage is a different matter. The conventional retail purchase unit is the ounce, fifty or more times the size of the conventional consumption unit, the joint. For a weekly user who doesn't share, an ounce is a year's supply.[12] A daily user might go through an ounce in a month or two; on the other hand, he might also buy a larger quantity to take advantage of bulk pricing. Heavy daily users are likely to buy in bulk, particularly if they are also resellers. If shortages were more frequent than they are now, consumers might tend to carry larger personal inventories against that risk.

The custom of sharing marijuana also acts as a kind of insurance policy against shortages; in effect, groups of users pool their personal inventories, thus spreading the shortage around. (Of course, this works both ways. If inexperienced users depend heavily on friends' supplies, the effects of shortages may be to reduce their consumption disproportionately and thus reduce the rate at which they are converted into regular users.)

Marijuana is also unlike heroin in that even those users who have serious drug abuse problems are not physiologically addicted. A period of forced abstinence does not appear to mark a crisis even for a heavily committed user. Thus few users are likely to be driven to treatment by the temporary unavailability of the drug.

Another important effect of a shortage of imported marijuana, were it to occur, might be to drive users to higher-priced, higher-potency domestic varieties whose distribution channels appear to be separate from those for commercial-quality imports. This possibility is discussed in the next section.

ENCOURAGING DOMESTIC PRODUCTION

If federal drug enforcement acts as a protective tariff benefiting the domestic marijuana trade, it will increase the fraction of marijuana consumed that is of very high potency (more than 6 percent THC by weight). This will have both costs and benefits from the viewpoint of controlling marijuana consumption.

On the one hand, it appears that high-potency, high-priced marijuana is not a perfect substitute on a potency-adjusted basis for lower-priced, lower-potency varieties. This may be either because users of the lower-potency drug find it difficult to adjust their consumption dosages, or because the effects of the two substances are qualitatively different.[13]

Whatever the reason, the lack of perfect substitutes presents consumers with a less attractive set of purchase opportunities, and may reduce (potency-adjusted) quantity consumed in consequence. (The shift in mix will act as an increase in the hedonic price index.[14]) The fact that a situation where only high-priced, high-potency marijuana is available is referred to by enforcement officials and users alike as a "shortage" suggests this effect at work. (If current prices in part reflect temporary scarcity premiums at the grower or dealer level on high-potency varieties, the relative price of the high-potency drug may tend to fall as its market share grows.)

But there are costs to be set off against this potential benefit. It is possible that the high-potency varieties have qualitatively different risks associated with them. Many of the most frightening health research findings about cannabis use—hallucinations and "flashbacks," for example—have been demonstrated only for use of hashish.

Moreover, the user literature reports that first-time and infrequent users of high-potency varieties tend to get more intoxicated than they expect or want to be, thus increasing rather than decreasing the frequency of excessive use. If the desired level of intoxication tends to move in the direction of levels experienced in the past, the effect of a shift toward domestic product will be to push marijuana users' habits in an unfavorable direction. The introduction of distilled spirits to a Europe used to wine, cider, and beer appears to have had such a bad effect.

Thus, while the predominance of high-potency marijuana might somewhat decrease the overall number of users, it would simultaneously increase the number of strongly committed users of a more dangerous drug.

NONMARKET EFFECTS OF CHANGES IN FEDERAL ENFORCEMENT

Drug enforcement can influence consumption in ways other than changing price and availability. The volume of enforcement activity can also communicate to users and potential users the effective level of social disapproval of a drug. However, the figures do not suggest that changes in federal activity are likely to influence public perceptions significantly. The

3,400 or so federal arrests for violation of the marijuana laws are barely a twentieth of the total marijuana sales arrests in the United States each year: state and local authorities arrest nearly 60,000 marijuana sellers. Arrests for simple possession are between 400,000 and half a million. While these arrests are unlikely to get the sort of press attention accorded a 50-ton boat seizure or the arrests and indictments after a major undercover operation, they strike the marijuana-using population much closer to home.

Were the federal government to eliminate enforcement and publicize this fact extensively, a message might indeed be sent to users and potential users that marijuana is less illegal than it used to be. Given the low visibility of federal enforcement even now, however, that is not at all the same as a quiet shift in relative enforcement shares. Odds are that such a policy change would pass largely unnoticed.

CHANGES IN USER BEHAVIOR

A doubling of federal marijuana enforcement would thus increase prices by not more than 13 percent and lead to a somewhat greater probability of local shortages in which ordinary "commercial" marijuana is unavailable though higher-priced, higher-potency *sinsemilla* is still for sale.

For most users, we have argued, the effects of price changes of this magnitude will be slight. The exceptions will be those users for whom marijuana consumption is a large budget item. These will be very heavy users who also have small incomes: either poor people or young users without earnings of their own. These, however, are precisely the populations whose marijuana consumption it is most desirable to reduce. This suggests that more vigorous enforcement, slight though its total effects might be, could nevertheless contribute significantly to curbing drug abuse among groups of especial social concern.

But the benefits to be derived from reducing marijuana use are reduced by the ability of marijuana users to adjust their habits to new conditions. There are a number of ways for heavy users with low incomes to react to increases in marijuana prices other than reducing their drug use. Many of them, in addition to defeating the drug abuse control objective of drug enforcement, have unpleasant aspects of their own. The same applies to users generally in times of shortage.

More Efficient Consumption

Marijuana is wasted in three ways: material is lost, scattered, or goes stale before being smoked; joints are not smoked down to the end; and THC goes off into the air rather than being absorbed by the lung. All of these losses can be reduced, with various degrees of inconvenience. It was argued earlier that moderate changes in marijuana price are unlikely to cause much of this kind of behavior, because the total price is still quite low. However, if physical shortage, rather than just an increase in price, is in question, or if we are considering users for whom marijuana is a major budget item, significant economies may be available: for example, switching from joints to the more efficient water pipes.

Such economizing behavior by users has no bad side effects of its own. It does, however, reduce the leverage of price increases or temporary shortages on the extent of marijuana intoxication.

Substitution

If marijuana is a substitute for other intoxicants, users may adjust to price increases or availability problems by switching to substitutes such as alcohol and phencyclidine (PCP or "angel dust").

Whether, on balance, this substitution is beneficial or harmful depends partly on the price and other characteristics of the substitutes that lead to more or less total intoxication and partly on the innate harmfulness of the substitutes.

Alcohol is modestly more expensive than marijuana. For users forced to cut back on marijuana consumption by price increases, alcohol will be an unattractive substitute. If marijuana is in shortage, however, users for whom intoxication is not a major budget item may switch. Presumably, such users will be switching from a more-preferred to a less-preferred combination of intoxication quality, intensity, side effects, and price; otherwise they would have been using alcohol in the first place. This may tend to reduce the total time spent intoxicated, which is presumably to the good. On the other hand, the acute behavioral risks of alcohol use—fights and automobile accidents—are much greater than those associated with marijuana. Trading hours of teenage marijuana intoxication for hours of teenage drunkenness is almost certainly a bad deal.

While alcohol is more expensive than marijuana, PCP is markedly less expensive. Some marijuana dealers are reported to adulterate inert material or low-potency marijuana with PCP to produce a low-cost, high-potency intoxicant, which they represent to buyers as very strong marijuana, and mental health workers sometimes see patients displaying the symptoms of PCP psychosis who report having used only a normal dose of marijuana.[15]

Marijuana price increases or shortages give dealers added incentives to adulterate marijuana with PCP or to sell PCP-laced leafy mixtures as marijuana. They also give users, particularly users who spend large fractions of their budgets on marijuana, added incentives to use PCP as a substitute.[16]

In the view of many, PCP is the single most dangerous illicit drug.[17] The risks of even a single experiment with PCP would more than offset the benefits of decreased marijuana use, even over an extended period, for any one user. Any substantial substitution of PCP for marijuana on a population basis would be an overwhelmingly bad trade from a social point of view. However, the volume of such substitution is a matter on which no published data exist.

Boosting Incomes and Reducing Other Expenditures

For marijuana users for whom increases in the price of marijuana represent a major financial burden, the alternative to cutting back consumption is to adjust the rest of their budgets by increasing income or reducing other expenditures.

For younger users, who are likely to constitute a major fraction of the population whose marijuana expenditures play an important role in personal budgets, boosting income in legitimate ways may be difficult. Illegitimate methods of boosting income might include theft and drug dealing. There is little evidence about theft as a source of funds for marijuana purchase, but the role of drug dealing in this regard is well established.[18]

Cutting back on other expenditures will be more or less possible and more or less harmful depending on what those expenditures are. An adolescent who buys fewer records or less fashionable clothes is one case; an adolescent who skips lunch at school is another. In general, though, the strategy of improving someone's welfare—even as externally perceived—by reducing his effective income (which is what a price increase for a budget item amounts to) seems problematic.

SUMMARY: INCREASED ENFORCEMENT AND CONSUMPTION PATTERNS

Where does this analysis leave our hypothetical decision maker? The doubling of enforcement resources he is considering would raise retail prices (in an upper-bound estimate) by 13 percent; this would result in a consumption decrease (again an upper-bound estimate) of 5 percent. Shortages would be difficult to create, and it would be nearly impossible to create shortages of domestic *sinsemilla;* this would push some users towards consumption of the more potent American product. Higher prices and shortages might also encourage more dangerous consumption patterns, exacerbate shifts to alcohol and PCP use, and encourage drug dealing and theft among adolescent users with low disposable incomes.

None of these deleterious side effects are foregone conclusions, however, and enforcement increase can reasonably be expected to cause a consumption decrease. Nevertheless, the decrease expected is sufficiently low—and the possibility of perverse effects on consumption sufficiently great—to make an increase of enforcement activity a poor use of public funds.

Similarly, an enforcement decrease would almost surely create an increase in consumption. One could expect, however, that the increase in effective consumption (consumption of

THC) would be noticably lower than the increase measured by weight of marijuana consumed. Moreover, more potent *sinsemilla* would not gain any market share; dangerous substitution behaviors would be discouraged; and the federal government would spend less money on enforcement.

NOTES

1. Peter Reuter, Gordon Crawford, and Jonathan Cave, *Sealing the Borders: The Effects of Increased Military Participation in Drug Interdiction* (Santa Monica, Cal.: RAND Corporation, January 1988), 118.

2. The imported marijuana market on the ton level was worth $2.1 billion, on the kilo level $4.4B and on the retain level $7.1B. The total retail market for both imported and domestic in 1982 was worth $10B.

3. These calculations use a ratio of imposed cost to price increase of 1 to 1.12. Cf. Polich et al., *Strategies for Controlling Adolescent Drug Use* (Santa Monica, Cal.: RAND Corporation, 1984) and Reuter and Kleiman, "Risks and Prices," in vol. 7 of *Crime and Justice: An Annual Review of Research,* ed. M. Tonry and N. Morris (Chicago: University of Chicago Press, 1986) for similar calculations.

4. Eugene M. Lewitt and Douglas Coate, "The Potential for Using Excise Taxes to Reduce Smoking" (unpublished paper, New Jersey Medical School and National Bureau of Economic Research, 1983).

5. This point was suggested by Tom Schelling.

6. I owe this point to Eric Rosenquist.

7. Very heavy marijuana users with limited incomes may already be spending so much of their budgets on marijuana that the income effect of a marijuana price increase pushes the price-elasticity of their demand up to something approaching unity. The ambiguous evaluative significance of this fact will be considered later in the chapter.

8. For the middleman who purchases marijuana from the fields, the cost of the physical plant is only a small fraction of his total costs. However, the value to him of having a reliable supplier who is never out of stock is great. Therefore, he is better off doing business with a supplier who produces an excess and charges incrementally more for what is actually purchased than with a supplier who charges less per plant but sometimes cannot meet the order. For the farmer, this is an instance of the general "inventory problem:" how much stock to keep if demand is uncertain. If the cost of keeping a stock too long is low, and the cost of being out of stock when a customer calls is high,

a storekeeper should keep an inventory that creates only a very small probability of running out, and therefore a high probability of being left with an excess.

9. The relationship between foreign supply and American consumption is discussed in Peter Reuter, "Eternal Hope," *The Public Interest* 79 (Spring 1985): 79–95.

10. L. D. Johnston et al., *National Trends in Drug Use and Related Factors Among American High School Students and Young Adults, 1975–1986* (Washington: National Institute on Drug Abuse, 1987), 52. This figure had decreased to 85 percent as of 1986.

11. John Kaplan, *The Hardest Drug: Heroin and Public Policy* (Chicago: University of Chicago Press, 1983), cf. 99–100.

12. Though marijuana potency decreases over time, some users do store the drug for that long. Marijuana can also be frozen or stored in nitrogen or carbon dioxide to retard deterioration.

13. William Novak, *High Culture* (New York: Alfred A. Knopf, 1980), 191–197, notes variation in consumer preferences for foreign and domestic varieties, though he does not specifally attribute these preferences to potency. Moreover, if the two varieties were perfect substitutes, we would expect them to have the same price. Instead, the potency-adjusted price of the more potent varieties appears to be somewhat higher than that of the imports, perhaps three times the price for twice the potency. This suggests that the two are imperfect substitutes.

14. Zvi Griliches, "Hedonic Price Indexes Revisited," *Price Indexes and Quality Change: Studies in New Methods of Measurement*, ed. Zvi Griliches (Cambridge, Mass.: Harvard University Press, 1971), 3ff.

15. David C. Hsia, private communication, based on experience at St. Elizabeth's Hospital, Washington, D.C.

16. Leon Hunt, in a private communication, reports PCP substitution as a consequence of marijuana price increases among adolescents in the Washington, D.C., suburbs.

17. See the papers in Robert C. Petersen and Richard C. Stillman, eds., *Phencyclidine Abuse: An Appraisal*, Research Monograph no. 21, (Washington: National Institute on Drug Abuse, 1978, reprinted 1984).

18. See Richard R. Clayton and Harwin L. Voss, *Young Men and Drugs in Manhattan: A Causal Analysis*, Research Monograph no. 59 (Washington: National Institute on Drug Abuse, 1981) which traces high rates of heroin use among heavy marijuana users to their participation in the drug-dealing trade.

7

The Dynamics of Marijuana Supply: Enforcement Effects on Illicit Markets[1]

TOTAL REVENUE AND NONDRUG CRIME INTENSITY

In principle, drug enforcement can create public benefits in three ways: by reducing drug consumption, by controlling the "spillover" of violence and corruption from illicit markets, and by limiting the problems of perceived fairness and the damage to public morale caused by notorious criminal wealth. Since new money spent on federal marijuana enforcement efforts will have little effect on drug consumption, its justification must come from its benefits in terms of "spillover" crime and perceived fairness. It is these concerns which are reflected in the argument that marijuana enforcement deserves high priority because of its connections with "organized crime." But it is far from clear that increased enforcement will ameliorate this complex of problems rather than exacerbate it.

PERCEIVED FAIRNESS AND PUBLIC MORALE

Criminal wealth is offensive to public spirit and to the notion that rewards flow to merit. The greater the wealth, the greater the offense. If, as argued in the previous chapter, marijuana is inelastically demanded around its current price, then moderate price increases will increase the total revenues of the industry. The 13 percent increse in price and 5 percent decrease in demand we estimated would increase total illicit revenues by about 9 percent. If demand were more inelastic, the revenue increase would be greater. Thus increased enforcement will tend to worsen the problems of public morale unless somehow the distribution of that wealth changes for the better.

One likely effect of increased federal enforcement is to increase the share of the market held by domestic growers. Since transactions in domestically grown marijuana tend to be smaller in size and more dispersed geographically than transactions in imported marijuana, domestic production is likely to support fewer very large organizations with great wealth concentrated at the top. Illicit incomes will also be spread widely across the country rather than concentrated at major importing centers such as South Florida.

But it is hard to see these differences as clear benefits. Is morale more or less damaged by having thousands of marijuana growers making substantial but not spectacular illicit incomes rather than scores of high-level dealers making millions? The answer is far from obvious. What is clear is that total illicit incomes rise as marijuana enforcement rises.

TOTAL REVENUE AND NONDRUG CRIME INTENSITY

Insofar as it increases illicit earnings, enforcement will tend to increase the opportunity and motivation for spillover crime as well: there is more money on the table to fight about. But it is necessary to ask as well how increased enforcement will influence the incidence of violence and corruption per dollar of illicit revenue—what might be called the nondrug crime intensity of the industry.

The effect of any enforcement change on nondrug crime intensity—nondrug crime per dollar of illicit revenue—will depend on whether it makes existing organizations more or less violent and corrupting, and whether it relatively advantages or relatively disadvantages the most violent and corrupting enterprises in the industry.

Drug enforcement against new entrants results in unequivocal benefits for experienced firms.[2] Increased enforcement also creates competitive advantages for the most enforcement-resistant firms for example, those with the greatest capability for other crimes, violence, and corruption even as it raises the total revenue of the illicit supply industry. Thus, a policy of strengthened enforcement both enlarges the revenue pie and gives the biggest slices to the most dangerous criminal organizations. Unless drug enforcement is specifically directed against the most skilled and ruthless criminals, it increases the returns for criminal ruthlessness and skill.

If both the total revenues of the illicit marijuana industry and its nondrug crime intensity increase with increasing levels of enforcement and decrease with decreasing levels of enforcement, then increases in federal marijuana enforcement will have perverse effects on the social harms associated with the illicit market in marijuana. It will encourage existing enterprises to improve their capabilities for using violence and corruption; it will increase the relative importance of existing firms with relatively heavy investments in such capabilities; and it will encourage enterprises that have developed such capabilities in other illicit industries to enter the marijuana trade.

THE NATURE OF SPILLOVER CRIME

During the course of business, marijuana traffickers commit a wide variety of crimes in addition to violations of the drug laws: tax evasion, bribery, obstruction of justice in all its forms, and all the degrees of assault and bodily harm, including homicide (directed at each other, at officials, and at potential witnesses). They are also attractive targets for robbery and extortion, both for each other and for nondrug criminals, sometimes including police, because they tend to have large amounts of portable wealth in the form of cash and drugs and because they cannot call for official help when threatened.

Spillover crime may be divided into two categories. The first category, "enforcement" crime, consists of crime among traffickers and between traffickers and civilians or police, which is generated by traffickers' attempts to avoid arrest and prosecution. The second category, "business crime," consists of crimes traffickers commit as part of business disputes and acquisitive crime (robbery and extortion) stemming from traffickers' inability to seek police protection.

A particularly important aspect of trafficking-related crime is the effect of drug trafficking on "organized crime," which raises the spillover and equity questions in the sharpest possible terms. Drug trafficking may provide opportunities for existing "organized crime" or help bring into existence new groups whose capabilities for predatory crime, vice trafficking, and corruption will overstep the bounds of, and perhaps even outlast, the particular illicit markets that spawned them. This problem combines elements of "business" and "enforcement" crime with other factors, and will be discussed in the next chapter.

"Enforcement" Crime

A business is designed to add value at low cost; the most successful business is the one that manages on a sustained basis to add the most value at the least cost. A conspiracy is designed to commit a crime and not get caught; the most successful conspiracy is the one whose members run the smallest risk of getting caught, either because the conspiracy avoids attracting enforcement attention or because its vulnerability to enforcement is low.

A drug-dealing enterprise, whether an individual or an organization, is both a business and a conspiracy. (Alternatively, it is a business subject to two special kinds of cost: the costs imposed by enforcement activity—loss of drugs, loss of other assets, imprisonment of principals and employees—and the costs of evading those actions.)

A business in a competitive market is in constant search for new customers, new suppliers, better products, less expensive ways of doing business. By contrast, a conspircy is superstitious, tied to established relationships and practices, because innovations increase the risk of getting caught; a new contact, a new participant, or a new activity is dangerous because it is not known to be safe.

Any illicit enterprise will be some mix of business and conspiracy, and the optimal mix will depend largely on external conditions, particularly on the level of enforcement pressure and the characteristics of competitors, suppliers, and customers. The more resources spent on enforcement, the higher the ratio of enforcement-related costs to ordinary costs of doing business will be. As this ratio rises, the more conspiratorial and the less businesslike the mix becomes.

An illicit business can deal with enforcement risks in three ways. It can absorb them and their effects and treat them as costs of doing business. It can avoid them by stealth. Or it can resist them actively by attempting to corrupt enforcement officials and by using violence and the threat of violence against officials and potential witnesses.

As the level of enforcement risk rises, absorption becomes less and less attractive relative to other strategies, and illicit business will make increasing use of stealth and of violence and corruption. That is why heroin is imported in much smaller units than cocaine, and why drug dealers are much more likely to shoot it out with police than are gamblers.

If the sentences handed out to lower-level dealers and the employees of high-level dealers are modest and relatively infrequent, then the costs associated with those sentences can be absorbed; the underling can be offered enough money to "stand up" and not inform on his supplier or his employer. But if arrests are frequent and the possible sentences are stiff, then neither past loyalty nor future reward can prevent the accused from making a deal with the government. The principals will then need to use violence, or at least its threat, to keep themselves out of prison.

The relationship between the level of enforcement pressure and the use of corruption is more ambiguous. A higher level of enforcement activity will increase the number of opportunities for on-the-spot bribes to avoid an arrest or seizure. At the same time, however, it may decrease the value and increase the risk associated with long-term corrupt relationships between trafficking groups and agents. The more agents and agencies involved in drug enforcement, the less the ability of any one agent to assure security for a dealer who pays off.

Strengthened enforcement directed at a particular illicit industry may also increase its importance in officers' eyes and thus their reluctance to participate in or tolerate corrupt connivance in it. Police who accept more from gamblers or after-hours bars are widely considered less corrupt than those who take money from drug dealers.

On the other hand, an increased level of enforcement increases the competitive advantage enjoyed by a successfully corrupting organization.

The same argument can be put in slightly different terms. Marijuana trafficking enterprises differ in the extent of their investment in organizational capabilities for the use of violence and corruption. The more of these capabilities an organization has, the more successful it will be at resisting enforcement. But such capabilities have costs, and those costs will only be justified at a sufficiently high level of enforcement pressure. Thus, the higher the level of enforcement pressure gets, the greater will be the optimal level of such capabilities for an organization to maintain.

"Business" Crime

Illicit firms with very different levels of capacity and willingness to use violence will find it difficult to do business together, since the less violent enterprise will find itself at the mercy of its more violent customer or supplier. This makes it hard for any firm to be far below the normal level of violence in its industry. Less obviously, it also makes it difficult for a firm to be far above the normal level of violence.

A firm with a reputation for unusual violence will encounter difficulty in finding transaction partners. If, however, it is for some reason able to estalish itself, its partners will be driven either to raise their own capacity for violence in self-defense, or to give way to new enterprises better able to hold their own in disputes with the new, more violent organization.[3] This effect is even clearer among competitors: the more violent firm will be able to threaten the less violent firm and that firm's customers as a way of increasing its market share. "Between one who is armed and one who is unarmed," Machiavelli tells his prince, "there is scorn in the one and suspicion in the other; it is not possible for them to work well together."[4]

If increased enforcement causes firms to acquire greater capacities for violence in the service of enforcement resistance, it will also tend, by raising the general level of armaments, to increase the role of violence in dispute resolution and competitive strategy. As the trade becomes more violence-intensive, the producers to whom violence is available at low cost gain competitive advantage vis-à-vis those for whom it is more expensive. This squeezing out of the relatively peaceful will make the trade even more dangerous. Criminal violence feeds on itself.

SECONDARY QUESTIONS

The above discussion raises three new questions:

- Why do we care about violence among criminals?
- Would reductions in enforcement increase competitive criminal violence as firms fought for increasing shares of a decreasing revenue base?
- How would changes in the marijuana industry influence the supply of labor for other criminal enterprises?

Violence among Criminals: Why Do We Care?

Corruption of law enforcement authorities is universally deplored, as is violence directed at ordinary citizens or at enforcement officials. Regarding criminal violence directed at criminals, however, there may be more ambivalence.

Even setting aside concern about the actual deaths and injuries involved (though criminals and their intimates may suffer as much as the rest of us when they are hurt or killed), criminal violence directed at criminals has bad effects on the surrounding population. Systematically unpunished violence— "getting away with murder"—is a particularly open challenge to the rule of law, and drug-related killings are one of the few categories of exceptions to the fairly high clearance rate for homicides. Even if the culprits were all punished and the victims were uniformly bad guys, the net result of a higher murder rate is likely to be increased fear among citizens at large; nobody wants to live in the "murder capital of the world."

It also seems plausible, though it would be hard to prove, that when criminals get into the habit of killing each other, they may be more prone to kill others as well. If rising murder rates encourage ordinary citizens to arm themselves, that too will tend to increase violent deaths among those who are not drug dealers.

Trafficking-Related Crime under Weakened Enforcement

It might be objected that decreases in enforcement pressure on an illicit market, if they led to decreases in the trafficking revenues available, might tend to increase the level of "business" violence as competitors struggled to maintain their revenues in a shrinking (in dollar terms) market. This could take the form of "turf wars" or of violence related to cartel formation and enforcement.

Neither possibility can be ruled out on strictly deductive grounds. Competitive violence has been known to result from industry shrinkage—perhaps the best-known example is the trucking industry violence of the early years of the Great Depression—and the relatively low level of enforcement activity under Prohibition did not prevent the sanguinary Beer Wars. Industries sufficiently illegal to prevent participants from calling the cops, but under slight enough enforcement pressure to allow relatively open operations without heavy physical security, might seem ideal targets for robbery, extortion, or attempts at cartel formation.

But the marijuana industry, at least at the levels at which federal enforcement interacts with it, does not seem to be well suited to the growth of "business" violence in the absence of enforcement pressure.

First, consider under what conditions shrinking revenues increase the incentives for competitive violence. The relevant condition would seem to be that the marginal value of a revenue dollar grows faster than the market shrinks, so that the importance of the game increases as the monetary stakes get lower. This condition will be characteristic of industries with high fixed costs, like the trucking industry, where the capital costs of the trucks must be met, or the garment industry, where a skilled workforce must be kept busy. In such industries an unexpected shrinkage in the overall market can convert competition for market share into a fight for survival, and both the trucking and garment industries have been characterized by violent attempts to gain competitive advantage or enforce minimum prices. Similar fixed cost pressures formed the backdrop for the switchgear industry price-fixing cases.

The marijuana market does not seem to be characterized by such a high level of fixed costs. As we have seen, "firms" rapidly form, grow, shrink, disappear, and reemerge, and even the roles of entrepreneur, agent, service provider, employee, buyer, seller, and broker, seem to be fluid. Neither the threat of fixed costs and idle assets leading to insolvency nor the opportunity provided by a well-defined industry structure seems to be present.

Moreover, the relatively high value-to-weight and value-to-bulk ratio of marijuana, though it encourages theft of the drug itself, tends to discourage competitive violence of the Beer Wars variety by eliminating tactically attractive targets. A marijuana distributor has no distillery, no large fixed warehouse, no trucks, no physical retail establishments on the model of speakeasies; he may not even have any permanent employees, and certainly has no army of brawny truckdrivers and deliverymen. Though marijuana is by far the bulkiest of the illicit drugs, it is fantastically more compact than alcohol: a $5 pint of whiskey and a $500 pound of marijuana weigh the same, net of packaging, and the marijuana occupies the same space as a six-pack of beer.

The relatively low-grade business violence of slashed tires, shattered windows, and burned trucks has no analogue in the marijuana trade, and systematic hijacking is infinitely more difficult because the goods are so much easier to conceal. If business disputes are to take a violent turn, there is no easy "ladder of escalation" to climb, no small change in the currency of unfriendly acts, and perhaps not even convenient proxies to

inflict and absorb personal violence while the principals ne-
gotiate. This should tend to reduce the frequency with which
disputes turn violent by inadvertence and limit business violence to those disputes where the principals are willing to run
the risks involved with trying to kill each other; such a dispute
will resemble a duel rather than a war.

In the absence of such "turf wars," decreasing revenues
should decrease the total number of violent disputes simply by
making the business less profitable.

Effects on Criminal Labor Markets

The analysis so far has ignored the effects of marijuana trafficking on the market for criminal labor and entrepreneurship
(except for the effects through the budgets of drug users). That
relationship is a tangled one, and little of significance can be
said a priori.

A simple static model would have criminals choosing their
next crime (or career segment) from the selection generated by
the laws and by enforcement strategies, balancing income and
risk: bank robbery is one choice, importing marijuana another.
A marijuana enforcement strategy that reduced the opportunities in the drug trade would then make additional labor available for other criminal enterprises. Even if—as seems likely—
the number of criminals varies with the opportunities available, so that the marijuana trade draws its labor supply partly
from other criminal endeavors and partly from the licit economy, it would still be the case (if the willingness to commit
crimes is unevenly distributed) that drug crimes compete with
other crimes in the labor market. If this were true, a flourishing
illicit marijuana industry would reduce the level of other
crimes requiring similar inputs of labor.

But if breaking the law is an individual and organizational
habit, or if having once been a criminal for a living reduces
one's licit opportunities and/or increases one's criminal opportunities, then a flourishing marijuana trade, by attracting honest citizens into the criminal labor force, will increase the
overall criminal labor force for the future. A subsequent decrease in marijuana-related criminal opportunities would then

create an underemployed criminal class and, thus, increases in nondrug crime.

OTHER MARKET EFFECTS OF INCREASED FEDERAL ENFORCEMENT

Dispersion

The process by which enforcement resources are allocated geographically tends to concentrate illicit industries. While the vast bulk of local jurisdictions have similar concentrations of police officers—between 1.5 and 3.0 police officers per 1,000 population—the value of drugs dealt per inhabitant varies enormously more widely. The number of police per drug transaction is consequently much smaller in areas where dealing is common than in areas where it is uncommon. Dealing is safest where it is most concentrated, because agents with targets to choose from are less likely to hit any individual target. Moreover, prosecutors and judges tend to view drug dealing cases more seriously where they are less frequent.

As a result, the growth of drug dealing in any area is a positive-feedback process: the relative safety provided by numbers will tend to attract dealers from less active to more active areas.

Federal drug enforcement activity is distributed far more unequally than is local police manpower, though still far less unequally than drug dealing itself. If DEA were allowed to distribute its agents to equalize the quality-adjusted cases per marginal agent-hour and thus to maximize its total case production, agents would be far more concentrated than they now are; it is a commonplce at DEA that any office with fewer than four agents ought to be closed, but that the congressional budget process will not allow it.

Initiatives like the South Florida Task Force, the Controlled Substances Units in selected U.S. Attorneys' Offices, and the Organized Crime/Drug Enforcement Task Forces (OCDE-TF) were designed in part to concentrate drug enforcement and prosecution resources more than they would otherwise have been. To some extent they have succeeded in doing so, but all such initiatives must deal with what might be called the "Model Cities Syndrome": the demand that the benefits of a concentration-of-resources program be widely distributed. Thus the South Florida Task Force became the National Narcotics Border Interdiction System, the Controlled Substances Units were folded into the general U.S. Attorney resource allocation process, and the OCDE Task Forces were transformed from the planned ten task forces in the ten biggest drug-dealing centers to twelve units "headquartered" in thirteen federal judicial districts,[5] with at least some resources in each of ninety-six districts in the country.

Still, the federal presence does bring the distribution of drug enforcement resources closer to the distribution of drug trafficking, and thus helps to counteract the tendency of drug dealing to concentrate itself. Increasing the total federal resource commitment to marijuana enforcement will thus tend to decrease the safety advantage enjoyed by marijuana dealers in the busiest markets.

For drugs where the supply control benefits of enforcement are paramount, this dispersive tendency may be valuable as it will tend to raise the overall costs of the industry. In the case of marijuana, however, the desirability of such dispersal is much less clear. It depends on whether the drug trade is more or less crime-intensive when it is geographically concentrated rather than dispersed, and on the shape of the damage function for trafficking-related crime. That is, if a ten-ton marijuana deal moves from Miami to a county on the Gulf Coast that has experienced little dealing in the past, is it more likely or less likely to involve violence and corruption? If the deal involved the same amount of violence and corruption, would that do more social harm in Miami or in rural Louisiana?

Neither available facts nor any clear line of reasoning suggest an answer to the question about crime intensity. On abstract grounds, one would expect the social damage done by violence to rise less than linearly with the number of incidents, because the first few incidents will each add more to fear and avoidance behavior than does each subsequent incident, and because fear and avoidance make up far more of the total social cost of violent crime than does actual injury. The same might be expected of corruption. In either case, however, there may be important perception-threshold effects making the first incident or two less important than some of the following ones.

On balance, then, the dispersive effect of federal enforcement would seem to be more likely to be harmful than helpful; the uncertainties, however, dominate.

Domestic Cultivation

As noted above, the growth of federal enforcement will tend to help domestic producers at the expense of importers. This will reduce average "firm" size in the illicit industry, which will tend to reduce concentrations of criminal wealth and power.

But increasing the share of domestic production has a disadvantage to be set against this advantage: domestic commercial production tends to be quite violence-intensive. Imported marijuana is relatively cheap at its moment of maximum danger, the point of importation. The cost of replacing a lost load is only about 7 percent of its resale price. Furthermore, the moment of danger is soon over; the goods are divided up, put on trucks, and scooted away.

Domestic cultivation, by contrast, involves a product whose value is largely intrinsic rather than transactional; *sinsemilla* is premium product, unlike imported marijuana, which gains value largely from having made it past the Coast Guard. For a domestic grower the loss of a crop is the loss of four to six months' labor. Unlike the importer, the grower cannot telephone Colombia for a replacement supply. In addition, the plants grow out in the open, vulnerable for months to enforcement agents and thieves alike.

As a consequence, the DEA domestic cannabis eradication report speaks of "widespread overt violence and the use of passive booby-trap devices" (including pipe bombs, punji boards, animal traps, and intrusion sensors). The U.S. Forest Service has complained repeatedly to the Justice Department that its Forest Rangers, timber licensees, and ordinary campers and hikers have been threatened or injured by marijuana cultivators using Forest Service lands.[6]

It is also widely believed within DEA that the apparent in-attention of local officials in marijuana-growing areas to wide-spread illicit cultivation is connected with corruption. (The alternative view is that local officials in depressed rural areas see little reason to disrupt the production of what may be a major cash crop.)

On balance, then, it is hard to see any dramatic net benefit on the illicit-markets side from increasing the share of domestic cultivation in the overall market.

SUMMARY: INCREASED ENFORCEMENT AND THE ILLICIT MARIJUANA MARKET

A 13 percent rise in marijuana retail prices and localized marijuana shortages, while slightly ameliorating the mari-juana consumption problem, will tend to concentrate the mar-ijuana trafficking problem. Increased enforcement would have two major effects in this regard: it would raise total illicit rev-enues in the marijuana market by raising the price of an ine-lastically demanded commodity and it would increase the nondrug crime intensity of the market by forcing the marijuana industry to become more conspiratorial and rewarding the most enforcement-resistant competitors. Any change in consump-tion that increased enforcement resources might bring about needs to be weighed against the increased criminal wealth, corruption of public officials, violence, and other crime that would accompany it.

NOTES

1. An earlier version of this chapter appears as "Drug Enforcement and Organized Crime" in *The Politics and Economics of Organized Crime,* ed. Herbert E. Alexander and Gerald E. Caiden (Lexington, Mass.: Lexington Books, 1984), 67–87.

2. See chapter 4.

3. Transactions with a dominant organized crime group may be an exception, if its behavior is predictable. The existence of such a group, whose members offer sponsorship and protection to illicit-market en-terprises and resolve disputes among them, may allow firms of dif-ferent capacities for violence to deal with each other, as long as both

are far less capable of violence than the dominant group. This set of problems is thoroughly discussed in Reuter, *Disorganized Crime*.

4. Machiavelli, *The Prince XIV*.

5. SDNY [Manhattan] and EDNY [Brooklyn] share "headquarters" designation.

6. Drug Enforcement Administration, *1984 Domestic Cannabis Eradication/Suppression Program Final Report* (Washington: Drug Enforcement Administration, 1984) lists multiple incidents of violence directed at enforcement agents. Mark McGowan, "The Domestic Cultivation of Marijuana in Hawaii" (unpublished extern paper, Stanford Law School, 1983), reports several killings of passersby who strayed too near marijuana fields there. The U.S. Forest Service has repeatedly asked the Justice Department for enforcement assistance against marijuana growers on Forest Service land who were threatening Forest Rangers, concession holders, and hikers.

8

Enforcement Effects on Corrupting Criminal Organizations

Let us return to the issue of the effect of marijuana enforcement on organized crime. An argument frequently made for more vigorous enforcement of the marijuana laws is that such enforcement can help "stop organized crime." (As will be noted below, this can mean either "help break up the Mafia" or "help prevent the growth of new enterprises that present, or may come to present, Mafia-like problems.") This argument suggests that the impact of marijuana enforcement on organized crime is taken to be a significant and independent consequence of the enforcement program, and should be examined separately from the program's overall effects on the illicit marijuana market.

We can think of organized crime as either a special aspect of the illicit-market problem or a distinct area of enforcement policy-making and activity with which marijuana policy interacts. From either perspective, the argument for increased marijuana enforcement as a weapon against organized crime needs to be examined in two ways. First, the theatrical connotation of homicidal Godfathers inherent in the term "organized crime" needs to be abandoned in favor of a definition that delineates characteristics of some criminal groups which make them the focus of special interest and concern.

Second, we need to determine how the market and nonmarket effects we have discussed—increases in market revenue, violence, and the market share of domestic producers—affect these groups. Once this is done, the argument that marijuana enforcement can help control organized crime begins to seem quite dubious.

DEFINING ORGANIZED CRIME

A definition of the term "organized crime" can be of any of three types. It can be descriptive: a hypothesis about the nature of the Mafia. It can be theoretical: a demarcation of an ideal type, like the firm of economic theory, about which precise reasoning is possible but whose relationship to actual phenomena remains to be explored. Or it can be normative: a sketch of the characteristics of certain actual or hypothetical criminal organizations that make them the worthy objects of a particular kind of social concern.

The test of a descriptive definition is whether it fits the facts. The test of a theoretical definition is whether it generates valuable insights, and whether the ideal type bears enough resemblance to some part of reality to make those insights meaningful. The test of a normative definition is whether it points out the right set of concerns. A great deal of the confusion that characterizes discussions of organized crime seems to stem from confusion among the types of definition, in particular from the difficulty in distinguishing propositions about the Mafia from propositions about all the entities that fit some theoretical or evaluative definition of organized crime.

The following discussion will proceed from a normative perspective, listing nine characteristics that make some criminal organizations "organized" and thus different from "ordinary" criminal enterprises. Of course, "distinctive" need not always mean "worse": for some purposes and from some perspectives, organized crime may be less noxious than disorganized crime. Nevertheless, the independent status of organized crime as a target of law enforcement activity will tend to limit the extent to which the "benefits" of organized crime can influence drug enforcement practice.

Formally, the discussion applies alike to "traditional" organized crime (the Mafia and its affiliates), to other multicrime organizations such as outlaw motorcylce gangs, and to marijuana-dealing enterprises that may take on similar characteristics. As a practical matter, very little federal marijuana enforcement involves the Mafia, though an occasional organized crime case turns out to have marijuana-related aspects. If increased marijuana enforcement is to be justified as organized crime strategy, it will have to be in terms of preventing new organized crime groups from arising out of the marijuana trade or improving our ability to control such groups as do emerge.

It should be noted that both because of the evaluative nature of the following discussion and the current low participation of the Mafia in the marijuana business, the term "organized crime" as used below can be somewhat misleading. Nevertheless, we retain it as a convenient shorthand for the kinds of criminal enterprises we take to be the concern of policies designed to "stop organized crime."

ORGANIZED CRIME CHARACTERISTICS AND THE EFFECTS OF ENFORCEMENT

Enforcement Resistance

Even if no other characteristic of organized crime groups were a source of concern, the extent to which such groups are organized to be enforcement-proof would in itself make them a particular enforcement target. This is because there is a natural tendency for persons associated with such groups to be apprehended and punished for a less than average fraction of their crimes. (This is analogous to the point that high-rate offenders deserve special enforcement attention because the ordinary workings of the system led to below-average rates of punishment per crime for high-rate offenders.[1]) That particularly prominent criminals should be punished for less than their share of crimes is offensive to the public sense of justice.

Beyond considerations of equity, each conviction and sentence of an organized crime participant also punishes, and prevents by incapacitation, a larger than average number of nondrug crimes. The extraordinary enforcement techniques with high costs or other undesirable features (wiretapping, "deep" undercover operations, assignment of new identities to dangerous criminals) often required to penetrate organized crime groups testify to the difficulty of making cases against them. Thus any organization with a design specialized to make it enforcement-resistant is a particularly valuable target both on grounds of equity and as a source of spillover crime.

But there is a paradox in trying to fight enforcement-resistant organizations with an increase in enforcement: the greater the level of enforcement, the greater the advantages enjoyed by enforcement-resistant enterprises.

This advantage enjoyed by successfully enforcement-resistant groups under heavy enforcement can be counteracted by enforcement designed specifically to go after such enterprises, either individually identified as such or with target selection criteria and techniques that allow enforcement-resistant groups to single themselves out. But these are the techniques of organized crime enforcement, not drug enforcement.[2]

Power and Wealth

Corruption is one form of the relationship between criminal enterprise and political power. Some criminal organizations may proceed beyond corruption to become the holders of substantial political power on their own. This is a problem both because such organizations and the politicians they work with are likely to be particularly undesirable decision makers and because the public reacts badly to the thought of being ruled by criminals and their friends. Regardless of whether or not criminal political power is an important source of enforcement resistance, it may still be an independent source of demoralization among enforcement agents and cynicism among citizens about enforcement agencies' diligence in pursuing big-time criminals.

The acquisition of great wealth by criminals poses comparable, though arguably less serious, problems for the functioning of the private economy and the perceived legitimacy of the economic system.

The total revenues available in the marijuana trade will, we have argued, increase as enforcement increases. However, a greater share of those revenues will go to small domestic cultivators and less to importers and distributors, who tend to engage in much larger transactions. Moreover, the optimal size of importation transactions, and thus possibly the optimal size of importing and distribution groups, may tend to shrink as the Coast Guard and Customs Service increase their interdiction efforts. Both the shift to domestic production and the shift to smaller import transactions will tend to reduce the size of the largest marijuana enterprises and, thus, the power and wealth of the most important marijuana traffickers.

Thus, increased marijuana enforcement, while increasing total revenue, may also increase the revenue share of small, independent, domestic growers at the expense of "organized" importers. This leaves it unclear whether increased federal marijuana enforcement will make the problem of criminal power and wealth more or less serious.

Intangible Criminal Capital

Criminals develop relationships of acquaintanceship and mutual trust, giving participants both knowledge of each other's characteristics and incentives to behave in other than immediately self-seeking ways in dealing with each other. These are at least as valuable in criminal enterprise as they are in ordinary business dealings; perhaps more valuable, insofar as they are substitutes for the open flow of market information and binding contracts. This intangible resource has been called "relational capital." A related resource is the skills that members of an organization build up in working together, including both more or less formal routines and operating procedures and interpersonal knowledge and skill. This second form of intangible resource might be called "organizational capital."

The more intangible criminal capital there is around, the greater the law enforcement effort required to keep crime at any given level, both because intangible criminal capital facilitates the business of lawbreaking and because it creates special problems for enforcement by giving participants particular incentives not to cooperate with the authorities. Imprisoning individuals who are foci of relational capital in criminal enterprise thus creates incapacitation effects beyond the crimes those individuals are prevented from committing, and the acquisition of such capital, independently of particular crimes, ought to be an object of deterrence.

For organizations narrowly specialized in marijuana trafficking, the intangible capital they build may contribute only to the supply of drugs and not express itself in spillover crime. With respect to more versatile groups and specialist groups that use greater than average violence and corruption, eliminating accumulations of relational and organizational capital will have both drug supply and spillover crime benefits. By pushing the marijuana trade in a more violent direction, increased enforcement will tend to increase the contribution of marijuana-based relational and organizational capital to spillover crime.

Reputational Capital

A reputation for being willing and able to use violence, like a reputation for trustworthiness, is an important form of intangible capital for criminals and criminal organizations. Being known to harm one's enemies may be even more valuable than being known to help one's friends. Once an organization has a well-advertised ability, or even a well-established but undeserved reputation, for the capacity and willingness to use violence, requests and offers from its members need not be accompanied by explicit threats in order to carry extortionate force. (For example: Sidney Korshak makes an enormous amount of money as a "labor lawyer" in part because his quiet suggestion that a position is "unreasonable" is understood to have Mob authority behind it; the solid-waste cartel in New York City appears to function without actual incidents of coercion.[3])

There thus can exist a class of extortionate crimes which, because no threat was ever uttered, are not provable even in principle. This brings enforcement resistance close to its zenith. Insofar as such reputations are developed in whole or part in the course of illicit-market dealings (as the organizational reputation of the Mafia was developed in part from the illicit alcohol trade) they represent one of the longest-lived varieties of spillover effect.

Holders of such valuably "bad" reputations[4] may be able to combine the reputational advantages of organized criminals with the lifestyles and the clear criminal histories of honest citizens. They thus have special opportunities to achieve "legitimate" power and wealth. This sort of blurring of the distinction between famous citizens and notorious criminals presents the equity problem of illicit markets in its most serious form.

Thus, on equity and spillover grounds, holders of "bad" reputations with legally clean hands deserve special enforcement attention for whatever provable crimes they do commit, and preventing the development of new centers of reputational capital ought to be a major objective of the organized crime side of marijuana policy. But if increasing federal enforcement will make the marijuana trade more lucrative and more violent, it will tend to increase, rather than decrease, the opportunities for the development of criminal reputational capital.

Provision of Dispute Resolution and Other Services to Illicit Enterprise

One function often performed by organized crime groups is the provision of dispute resolution and contract enforcement services to criminals, thus ameliorating some of the central disadvantages of illicit enterprise. Disrupting the entities that provide these services should therefore tend to make illicit enterprise less efficient from the perspective of its participants, and thus, other things equal, to reduce its scope.

If marijuana dealers were heavy consumers of such services, organized crime enforcement might help restrict the marijuana supply; if drug-trafficking revenues help maintain organizations that provide such services to other criminal enterprises, drug enforcement activities against such groups will help reduce the spillover problem, while drug enforcement activities against their competitors may exacerbate it. However, since the ability to provide such services will be correlated with enforcement resistance, a general increase in marijuana enforcement will tend to help, rather than hurt, the groups one would want to eliminate.

The same analysis applies to other service provider roles of organized crime groups, for example the role of the loan shark industry as a parallel financial market.

Economies of Scale in Lawbreaking

Some forms of lawbreaking may be possible, or worthwhile to the participants, only if carried out on a sufficiently large scale. If this is so, the creation or maintenance of large criminal enterprises will be a problem distinct from the criminal activity that creates or maintains them. If the sheer size of the marijuana market allows some participants in it to achieve economies of scale in other criminal enterprise, attacks on such groups will help reduce the spillover effect, while attacks on their competitors will make it worse.

If a substantial number of marijuana enterprises are large enough to achieve economies of scale in other criminal lines, the net spillover effect of increasing or decreasing enforcement against them as a class is indeterminate; there is no a priori reason to think that four firms with $50 million in annual revenues are either more or less dangerous than one firm with $200 million in revenues.

Here again, the increase in total revenues in the marijuana trade will work against our objectives, but the diversion of revenues from importers and distributors to domestic producers will work for them.

Corruption

The corruption of enforcement authorities is among the most feared spillovers from the vice markets. It is also a source of enforcement resistance and, as such, one reason that the organized crime enforcement effort absorbs such enormous resources.

As noted above, an increase in enforcement will have complicated effects on the overall level of corruption, but will tend to increase the advantages enjoyed by organizations successful at systematic corruption. It is this sort of corrupt relationship, rather than the one-shot bribe, that makes organized crime a special target of enforcement. If the growth of new enterprises with skill at corruption is the concern, an increase in federal marijuana enforcement seems unlikely to be helpful.

Violence

Violence is like corruption: both a problem in itself and a source of enforcement resistance. Here the analysis is less ambiguous than in the case of corruption: increased marijuana enforcement is likely to increase the level of violence and to cause trafficking organizations to build organizational capacities for the use of violence. It will make the marijuana trade more likely, rather than less likely, to spawn new organized crime groups.

SUMMARY: ENFORCEMENT AND ORGANIZED CRIME

In a paper entitled, "What is the Business of Organized Crime?" Thomas C. Schelling suggests that, under quite plausible conditions, the existence of organized crime might be of service to the supression of vice by keeping prices higher than they would otherwise be.[5] The present line of argument suggests the converse: that government efforts to suppress vice, and in particular the marijuana traffic, are likely to encourage the growth of organized crime.

Does this mean that the Mafia, if it were well advised, would use its remaining political influence on behalf of increased federal marijuana enforcement, or that the Hell's Angels ought to contribute to the Mothers Against Marijuana, or that the toughest organizations currently in the marijuana traffic ought to welcome increased attention from DEA? There seems to be a paradox here that needs to be untangled on several levels.

First, enforcement is not a zero-sum game between criminals, or organized criminals, and the rest of us. It is not the well-being of drug dealers that we fear, but their dollar revenues, their accumulated wealth, and their ability and incentive to use violence and corruption. It is possible to make the organized crime problem worse without making the organized criminals better off.

Second, organizations currently in the marijuana business must be distinguished from organizations that might be drawn into it as increased enforcement makes their existing capabilities for violence and corruption more useful in it. Even the toughest existing marijuana firms might find themselves made worse off if enforcement picked off their milder competitors, forced the remainder to invest more in enforcement resistance, and lured still rougher organizations into the trade. New entrants, on the other hand, presumably enter because it is in their interest to do so, and thus necessarily expect to come out ahead.

Third, some criminals get caught, while others do not. To some extent, this is a random process, or at least appears random until the outcomes are known. A lottery where some of the proceeds go to the organizers makes lottery ticket buyers as a group poorer, but it makes the winners richer. Similarly, increased enforcement could increase the overall well-being of organized crime participants as a group, and thus the lifetime expected-value welfare of each individual who chooses to try his hand at high-level crime, but decrease not only the dollar wealth but also the overall welfare of the unskilled or unlucky losers.

Finally, if risk aversion, skill at evading punishment, and willingness to do time are unequally distributed across the population of potential lawbreakers, those who are least risk averse, most highly skilled, and least bothered by a stretch in prison may be net beneficiaries, even in an expected-utility sense, from increases in enforcement that improve their market position relative to more cautious, less gifted, and more liberty-loving competitors.[6]

NOTES

1. Mark Moore et al., *Dangerous Offenders: The Elusive Target of Justice* (Cambridge, Mass.: Harvard University Press, 1984).

2. For a fuller discussion of this point, see chapter 9.

3. Peter Reuter, "Racketeers as Cartel Organizers," in *The Politics and Economics of Organized Crime,* ed. Herbert E. Alexander and Gerald E. Caiden (Lexington, Mass.: Lexington Books, 1984), 49–66.

4. Peter Reuter, *The Value of a Bad Reputation: Cartels, Criminals and Barriers to Entry* (Santa Monica, Cal.: RAND Corporation, 1982).

5. *Journal of Public Law* 20 (1971): 71–84. Reprinted in Thomas C. Schelling, *Choice and Consequence* (Cambridge, Mass.: Harvard University Press, 1984) 179–194. The discussion involves only gambling, but the structure of the analysis would seem to apply to drugs as well.

6. See the exchange on this last point between Mark Moore, "Policies to Achieve Discrimination in the Effective Price of Heroin," *American Economic Review* 63 (May 1973): 270–277, and A. Michael Spence, "A Note on the Effects of Pressure in the Heroin Market," Harvard Institute of Economic Research Working Paper 588, November 1977.

9

Implementation and Ancillary Issues

One important issue remains for the consideration of our hypothetical decision maker in 1982. The analysis of the previous chapters has argued that increasing federal marijuana enforcement would likely exacerbate the total marijuana "problem"; moreover, it would do so at increased taxpayer expense. An enforcement reduction, conversely, would reduce governmental expense without appreciably worsening the marijuana problem—and even with the result of alleviating it in some important ways.

However, our analysis thus far has assumed the federal government's ability to vary enforcement levels continuously and at will. This is not manifestly the case, to say the least. This chapter therefore will examine the feasibility of adjusting 1982 marijuana enforcement levels downward and towards an emphasis on marijuana-importing and -growing firms that exhibit characteristics of organized crime.

THE NECESSITY FOR RESIDUAL ENFORCEMENT

The argument to this point has tried to establish that a reduction in federal marijuana enforcement from its current level would have, on balance, beneficial effects. But that does not

...ply, and it is probably not the case, that reductions would continue to be beneficial down to, or very near, zero.

First of all, it is politically, organizationally, and even operationally difficult to prevent law enforcement agencies from enforcing laws on the books, particularly when some of the forbidden activity is either quite flagrant or likely to be encountered in the course of other enforcement activity. There are limits to the effective range of police discretion: agent morale suffers if agents must consistently witness violations of the law without acting to stop them. The public is also unwilling to tolerate flagrant and unpunished violations. Thus, unless marijuana were to be legalized—an option discussed in chapter 11—some level of enforcement is almost inevitable.

In addition, the argument that marijuana consumption is only weakly sensitive to the level of federal enforcement rests on the assertion that likely variations in federal enforcement will not strongly influence public perceptions about the risks and social status of the drug and its traffickers. That assertion is probably true only within some range; even if a 50 percent reduction in the number of headlines of the form "Feds Nab Huge Pot Shipment" had no measurable impact on public attitudes about the drug, the elimination or virtual elimination of such headlines might have a substantial impact, by bringing the drug closer to a status one might call "effective legalization." As we argue below about legalization, the elimination or near-elimination of federal marijuana enforcement carries costs and risks discontinuous with those of reducing enforcement from its current level to some lower, but still noticeable, level.

MARIJUANA ENFORCEMENT AS AN ORGANIZED CRIME CONTROL EFFORT

We have seen that some marijuana-trafficking organizations pose the mix of spillover crime and equity effects that characterize organized crime as a special set of enforcement targets, and some individuals and organizations already identified as organized crime targets engage in marijuana dealing. The residual marijuana enforcement strategy should create competitive disdvantages for the most organized-crime-like marijuana traffickers and take advantage of any vulnerabilities inherent in the marijuana-dealing activities of existing organized crime groups. Except in the extraordinary circumstances of, for example, the "French Connection" case, where organized crime groups are the low-cost suppliers to a particular drug market, the operating routines and management measures characteristic of drug enforcement agencies will not, in general, be effective in searching out organized crime targets. Drug enforcement agents and groups are measured by their productivity of good cases, where a good case is one against a substantial trafficker or trafficking organization (G-DEP Class I). But if, as argued above, organized crime groups are specialized in enforcement resistance, then enforcement activity concentrated on them will yield relatively fewer good cases.

A comparison of DEA with the organized crime effort of the FBI is instructive here: while 1,700 DEA agents open and close cases at a rate of 8,000 per year and maintain more than 14,000 active case files,[1] the roughly 2,000 agents in the FBI Organized Crime Program spend about three-quarters of their time on the Mafia, with an estimated 500–1,000 "made" members and another 2,000 to 3,000 "close associates."[2] One reason that DEA has shied away from wiretaps and electronic "bugs" is that electronic surveillance, though ideal for untangling large conspiracies and producing evidence against persons who arrange to be absent from crime scenes, is a notoriously manpower-hungry approach to investigation; a wiretap on a single site requires at least eight, and more likely twelve, full-time agents while in operation, not counting the costs of enhancing, transcribing, and cross-indexing the resulting recordings.[3]

A true combined organized crime and marijuana enforcement effort would therefore have to build an institutional tolerance for low numbers of cases and develop an organizational culture that understood success in terms of very occasional but very big successes.

It would also have to emphasize nondrug crime intensity—in particular violence, corruption, and the obstruction of justice—rather than drug volume in choosing targets worthy of such concentrated effort. Once chosen, the targeted organizations and individuals would have to become the focus of investigative effort to the virtual exclusion of other organizations not meeting the program's criteria.

Such an organizational culture would find it difficult to survive within DEA unless its agents, lilke the organized crime agents in the FBI, could count on having very long career segments within it; otherwise, participation in the organized crime effort would so damage agents' promotional potential that ambitious agents would resist taking part in organized crime cases. That was precisely the fate of the DEA CENTAC (Central Tactical Unit) program, which drafted large groups of agents from different DEA components to devote themselves over periods of many months to pre-identified target organizations. DEA headquarters was highly satisfied with CENTAC operations, which claimed a success rate of nearly 100 percent, but field agents and their supervisors disliked the program intensely. It was proverbial within DEA that one CENTAC assignment would set your career back by two years, and that two such assignments would wreck it almost beyond repair.

The FBI Organized Crime Program has another resource for which no current analogue exists in the drug prosecution world: a dedicated set of prosecutors sharing its long-term, big-case focus. Indeed, one way to view the FBI Organized Crime Program is that it was called into being by the creation of the Organized Crime Strike Forces, consisting of career-service Criminal Division prosecutors. Neither the skills for long, multidefendant, document-intensive trials nor the patience to wait until the entire case is ripe is likely to be common among short-term prosecutors with external reputations to make.

In addition, the Strike Forces and their career-service members have both the time and the incentives to develop long-term trust relationships with the agents assigned to organized crime cases. Given the built-in professional tensions between agents and prosecutors, which are aggravated by differences in ethnicity, class background, education, and career options after government service, such relationships are not easy to come by.

In particular, agents resist sharing information with lawyers who may later, as members of the defense bar, oppose them.

Of course, the revolving door swings for Strike Force attorneys as well as for Assistant U.S. Attorneys, but it swings more slowly, and ex–Strike Force attrorneys are more likely to represent white-collar defendants than accused Mafiosi. Federal drug prosecutors are much more likely to become drug defense attorneys; such, at least, is the common wisdom.

One place to attempt to create an institutional capacity for marijuana / oranized crime investigations would be within the Organized Crime Program itself, with FBI Organized Crime agents and Strike Force prosecutors. However, the very success of that program against its primary targets—the Mafia and its associates—has made its participants highly resistant to demands that they take on outlaw motorcycle gangs, Chinese Tongs, Japanese Yakuza, Colombia "Cocaine Cowboys," and other "nontraditional" criminal organizations. As organizations and as individuals, they are now engaged in a high-prestige activity at which they can have consistent and demonstrable success. From the perspective of the organizational health of the Strike Forces and the FBI Organized Crime Program, a change in their mission definition has many more risks than it has potential rewards.

Moreover, the U.S. Attorneys, whose status as presidential appointees in their own right, relationships with senators of the president's party, and statutory roles as the chief federal law enforcement officers of their districts (backed by the power to sign, or refuse to sign, indictments) all give them considerable influence, tend to be jealous of the quasi-independent roles of the Strike Forces and vigorously resist any expansion of Strike Force jurisdiction. That the prosecutors in the Organized Crime / Drug Trafficking Task Forces are Assisstant U.S. Attorneys reflects in part the desire of the U.S. Attorneys not to see the Strike Forces expand or to see any similar institutions established. While the Strike Forces and the FBI Organized Crime agents with whom they work will continue to pursue marijuana cases involving their traditional targets in the Mafia, it would be difficult to engage them in pursuit of other organized-crime-like targets in the illicit marijuana industry.

Nor would it be at all easy to create a parallel set of prosecutorial institutions to do just drug cases involving "nontra-ditional" organized crime; in addition to the initial political resistance from the U.S. Attorneys, such a program would gen-erate continuous resentment and turf battles with drug units in the U.S. Attorney's Offices. The increasing professionali-zation of drug prosecutors within the Attorney's Offices means that the dearth of big-trial skills within the districts is a di-minishing problem, but the problems of resource limits, im-patience, and the revolving door are likely to remain and to create continuing problems for the organized crime / drug en-forcement effort. By all accounts, the prosecutors assigned to the OCDE Task Forces are not developing the sense of sepa-rateness and special mission within the U.S. Attorneys' Offices that would make them resemble the Strike Forces.

How successful either DEA or the FBI could be in developing an effective marijuana / organized crime investigative capacity in the absence of a corresponding set of institutions on the pros-ecutive side remains to be seen. But the argument for either locating it within the Organized Crime Program of the FBI or creating a separate unit within DEA or FBI seems strong.

IMPLEMENTING A RESOURCE CUTBACK

A high-level decision to redirect federal drug enforcement resources away from marijuana would not be self-executing. Since none of the agency budgets involved is drawn up on a drug-by-drug basis, there is no marijuana line item to cut.

Before the reorganization that put DEA under the admin-istrative authority of the director of the FBI, DEA did maintain internal targets for the resource shares to be devoted to each of the four major drug categories: heroin and the other opiates, cocaine, the "dangerous drugs," and cannabis (marijuana and hashish). The targets were a holdover from the period when DEA, following the lead of the White House Office of Drug Abuse Policy, had formally ranked marijuana at the bottom of a five-tier national priority-ranking system, with heroin at the top. Though systematically missed in practice (through the late 1970s, heroin investigations were in chronic shortfall and cocaine cases in chronic surplus), at least the targets expressed a headquarters intention about relative priorities among drugs.

However, one of the first administrative actions of the post-merger DEA management was the abolition of drug-by-drug resource targets. Nevertheless, abolishing the priorities and the targets did not entirely erase the attitudes of DEA managers and agents that marijuana cases were, on the whole, of secondary importance compared to cocaine and (particularly) heroin.

In any case, the overall targets were never as powerful in shaping the behavior of lower-level organizational units and of individual agents as the G-DEP case and violator ranking system. The excess of cocaine cases and the shortfall of heroin cases reflected the fact that the G-DEP criteria made, and still make, Class I cocaine cases far easier to find than Class I heroin cases. During FY 1984, for example, when the drug targets had been abolished and cocaine's share of total man-hours had soared to almost 45 percent, cocaine investigations were producing Class I and II arrests at a rate of 2.8 per 1,000 hours of investigation, as compared with 1.6 "quality" arrests per 1,000 hours of heroin investigation.

Marijuana work was even more productive, as DEA measures productivity: 4.0 Class I and II arrests per 1,000 investigator-hours.[4] Changing the quantitative criteria under the G-DEP system to make fewer marijuana cases Class I or requiring the presence of major nondrug charges (violence or corruption) in order to qualify marijuana cases as Class I would reduce individual and unit incentives to work on marijuana cases. Of the investigative work-hours allocated to particular marijuana cases (rather than to the General File) about five in six (300,000 of 365,000) involved Class I cases.[5]

Even with the current G-DEP rankings, DEA spends only about 15 percent of its agent-hours on marijuana. Marijuana's share of DEA's other major scarce resource is even smaller: only 4 percent of funds used for the purchase of evidence or information (PE/PI or "buy money") went to marijuana cases. The sums involved are not large—total PE/PI was less than $7 million compared with the $327 million DEA budget—but PE/PI money is both an important resource in chronic relative undersupply and, since its distribution is far more tightly centrally controlled than is the allocation of investigative manpower, a measure of headquarters priorities.

The FBI, on the other hand, appears to spend far more of its effort on marijuana. FBI uses a simpler case-ranking system than does DEA: a case is either a Priority case or it is not. G-DEP Class I and Class II drug cases, but no others, are given Priority treatment; and the FBI, without DEA's history of considering the "hard" drugs as its main mission, may take the case classifications more seriously. If so, changing the case-ranking system would have more influence on FBI behavior than on DEA behavior.

Organizational and Geographic Resource Allocation

However, changing resource allocations geographically and among agencies is likely to have more influence on the distribution of enforcement attention than changing priority systems within agencies. The Customs Service and the Coast Guard spend far more of their effort on marijuana than does DEA; indeed, much of DEA's limited marijuana effort goes into processing Coast Guard cases. This is not because Customs and the Coast Guard decided to specialize in marijuana, but because of the nature of marijuana smuggling and the agencies' role as pursuers of dedicated drug-smuggling craft.[6] Therefore, moving resources from Customs and the Coast Guard to DEA and reallocating the Customs budget away from criminal investigations and toward inspection will move resources away from marijuana cases.

Geographic reallocation works analogously. Resources in Florida are more likely to be used in marijuana cases than are resources in New York. (The Miami DEA office spent more than one-quarter of its investigative time on marijuana; New York less than one-twentieth.)[7]

Unless one favors (as I would) increasing the resources applied to heroin and the "dangerous drugs" at the expense of both marijuana and cocaine, the effectiveness of a policy of organizational and geographic reallocation is limited by the fact that marijuana and cocaine overlap in terms of smuggling routes and techniques, so that a reduction in the share of resources going to marijuana is likely to reduce the share going to cocaine as well. Moving resources away from marijuana while maintaining the cocaine effort at its current resource share would require detailed intervention in the management of the individual agencies.

Establishing Prosecutive Priorities

Another important way one might influence both the level of marijuana enforcement and the mix of marijuana cases between pure drug cases and cases with organized crime elements would be to establish a formal case-weighting system for prosecutors.

Such a system, designed in a way that tended to downgrade "pure" marijuana cases, would produce two kinds of effects: prosecutor time would move away from marijuana cases toward other drug cases, and investigators, finding that their marijuana cases were receiving less prosecutive attention than their other drug cases, would be less eager to work marijuana investigations.

(The success of the Strike Forces, under orders from Washington, in discouraging the FBI from bringing gambling cases under the Organized Crime program illustrates the indirect influence of prosecutive decisions over investigative behavior. This success is particularly notable because the element of persuasion was largely absent; the FBI strongly resisted, and continues to bitterly regret, the move away from gambling.)

Unlike some of the steps discussed above, prosecutive priorities could be established entirely within the Justice Department. However, any such move would encounter strong resistance from line prosecutors and the heads of drug units, who have successfully resisted such efforts in the past.

The downgrading of marijuana cases would not be the focus of resistance; indeed, this might be generally agreed on. But the principle of case ranking, with its implication that each case is not sui generis and that prosecutive efforts can be measured and prosecutors assigned annual "scores," is perceived by many prosecutors as both an insult to their status as members of a learned profession and a threat to their personal autonomy. Prosecutors value the status differences that separate them from agents as much as agents resent them. One symbol of those differences is the fact that agents have their accomplishments counted and measured while prosecutors have theirs discussed.

Establishing a prosecutive case evaluation system could therefore be an extremely powerful way of changing resource allocations, and of changing the mix of cases within drug categories as well. However, a great investment of time and authority on the part of the top management of the Justice Department would be needed to put such a system in place.

Given prosecutors' strong distaste for paperwork, a prosecutive priority system would need to be simple to be workable at all. This would virtually dictate basing it on the G-DEP system, by starting with the G-DEP violator class, upgrading or downgrading for the drug involved, and then applying an additional set of criteria based on nondrug offenses involving violence or corruption. As G-DEP illustrates, such systems work only imperfectly, with considerable "creative writing" and organizational politics going into the rankings of individual cases. But as long as they retain some credibility and as long as individual and organizational rewards are based on them, they can influence behavior profoundly.

Budgeting Prison Cells

Another approach to influencing prosecutive behavior would be to attempt to budget prison space. As suggested above, the enormous growth in drug enforcement over the last three years threatens to cause a massive federal-prison-crowding crisis by adding a large number of additional inmates to a system already well over its capacity. It is possible that Congress will choose to fund enough prison cells to hold all the convicted drug offenders: the capital cost of doing so would be approximately $450 million and the annual operating cost around $180 millon, not outrageous sums.[8] But it is equally possible that Congress will refuse to do so, or that budgetary, organizational, or construction lags will leave the federal prison system intolerably overcrowded for several years. The abolition of federal parole removes what might have been an escape valve for the population pressure on that system.

In the face of such pressure, the Justice Department would either have to attempt to manage the population crunch on its own or trust the judges to ration themselves. One approach to managing prison population would be to establish target aggregate prison accruals by federal judicial district (U.S. Attorney's Office) and by category of crime. Though it may be difficult for a prosecutive office to increase the aggregate imprisonment in its cases, decreasing the total is far easier; it can be done by bringing less serious charges, offering more generous plea agreements, and reducing recommended sentences after conviction.

Moreover, Justice Department top management could use the allocation of Assistant U.S. Attorney positions to encourage adherence to budgeted imprisonment totals, since reducing an office's complement of prosecutors would directly reduce the number and complexity of its future case filings as well as expressing departmental disapproval of an office that had overspent its previous cell budget.

Such a drastic interference in the autonomy normally accorded to U.S. Attorneys could be justified only in the face of a generally recognized crisis. In those circumstances, the additional step of attempting to manage the use of prison space by crime as well as by office might cause little additional controversy. It would act far more powerfully than would the establishment of prosecutive case rankings to influence the allocation of all resources by drug and by the presence or absence of important nondrug charges.

NOTES

1. Drug Enforcement Administration, Annual Statistical Report FY 1984, (Washington: Drug Enforcement Administration, 1984), 6.

2. These are unreliable estimates of unpublished numbers, but are believed accurate to a tolerance of plus or minus 50 percent.

3. DEA, *Annual Statistical Report,* 151, lists only eighty-three Title

III intercepts for FY 1984 where DEA was the primary requesting agency, about 8 percent of the federal total. Of those, twenty-five were in New York, the city where drug investigations are most likely to involve the Mafia.

4. DEA, *Annual Statistical Report,* 168–172. Note that field offices are competitively ranked on this productivity measure.

5. DEA, *Annual Statistical Report,* 97.

6. Within the Customs Service, the inspectors who search passenger luggage and freight are far more likely to intercept heroin and the "dangerous drugs" than are the special agents who work primarily airplane and boat cases.

7. DEA, *Annual Statistical Report,* 97–102.

8. A rough estimate of 9,000 additional prisoners multiplied by $50,000 capital cost and $19,800 annual operating cost.

SUMMARY: A MARIJUANA POLICY FOR 1982

Let's again return to 1982, and ask how the new administration should be advised to best "do something" about America's "marijuana problem." A consideration of the possible impact of a dramatic increase in enforcement resources shows that even a doubling of those resources cannot raise marijuana prices by more than 13 percent. Neither can it impose long-term marijuana shortages, although it can create localized shortages of imported product, leaving only higher-potency domestic *sinsemilla* available in some areas.

If it were to do these things—increase price and create localized shortages—the effects would likely be small and might even be counterproductive. Domestic marijuana use would increase at the expense of the less potent imports, but marijuana's low elasticity of demand makes it unlikely that overall consumption would decrease significantly. This creates a situation in which only slightly fewer people are using a significantly more potent product. Furthermore, some users for whom marijuana is a significnt budget item, especially minors and the poor, would be encouraged to seek more dangerous substitutes, especially alcohol and PCP.

Conversely, enforcement reductions are not likely to significantly worsen the drug abuse situation: the low cost imposition of enforcement (10 percent of retail price) does not suggest that marijuana prices would significantly drop, and a shift in enforcement resources would likely pass unnoticed, without changing public perceptions of the drug.

Enforcement increases are, moreover, likely to have perverse effects on the social harms associated with the illicit marijuana market. Total revenue available to drug dealers will increase and those enterprises with the greatest capability for violence and corruption will prosper, since these enterprises will be the most competitive in the new, more dangerous business environment. Increasing the level of marijuana enforcement will also tend to increase the violence intensity of the marijuana trade per dollar of revenue even as it increases the number of dollars involved, by rewarding those competitors most skilled at enforcement resistance.

Here, too, enforcement reductions promise the opposite effect. Without significantly exacerbating consumption, reducing enforcement would not only save the government money, but would reduce the advantages enjoyed by enforcement-resistant criminal groups, reduce total criminal revenue, and reduce marijuana-related violence and crime.

In addition, such a reduction of enforcement would not have the effect of somehow aiding or abetting "organized crime." Despite the popular view of drug enforcement as a bulwark against the creeping wealth and power of "organized crime" groups, analysis of any reasonable construal of the term shows that reducing enforcement would at the least harm organized crime as much as it would help it.

This is not to suggest a reduction of enforcement to zero or a public announcement of lowered enforcement levels. Rather, enforcement costs should be lowered by a quiet attempt to reduce (but not eliminate) the investigation, prosecution, and incarceration costs associated with marijuana enforcement. This might prove to be organizationally and bureaucratically difficult, especially given the absence of a marijuana budget line-item, but there does exist a series of steps which could move the bureaucracy in that direction.

For an administration committed to an intensified war on drugs, a counterintuitive policy of lowered marijuana enforcement would be difficult to accept. Nevertheless, analysis shows that in the case of the marijuana problem, the "intuitive" policy—spending more to achieve one's goal—actually leaves one more distant from that goal than a policy of spending less. It is important not to allow the marijuana problem to be equated with weight of marijuana consumed, and to emphasize that the aggregate harm caused by the drug can be lessened by policies leading to small increases in that figure. Significantly reducing enforcement levels is just such a policy.

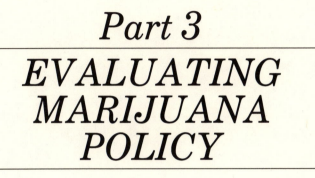

Part 3
EVALUATING MARIJUANA POLICY

10

Evaluating Marijuana Enforcement, 1982– 1986

From the perspective of our hypothetical 1982 decision-maker, a substantial increase in marijuana enforcement appears to be a bad choice. Our analysis of the 1982 marijuana industry suggests that such an increase would have only limited benefits in terms of reduced consumption and probably perverse affects on the social damage done by the illicit market.

Actual decision-makers decided differently. Between 1982 and 1986, the federal marijuana enforcement budget grew from $423 million to $636 million, an increase of 50 percent (23 percent in constant dollars).[1] This gives us some chance to compare the predictions about increased enforcement discussed in Part 2 with actual experience.

That comparison is necessarily imprecise. This is both because of the difficulty of finding precise and relevant data, and, more profoundly, because the real world does not provide a laboratory in which hypotheses can be tested *ceteris paribus*. We have no way of knowing what would have happened in the absence of the enforcement buildup. The period from 1982 to 1986 witnessed rapid economic, demographic, and cultural changes independent of the level of Federal marijuana enforcement spending and not accounted for in our prospective model. Thus, strictly speaking, the events of those years can neither confirm nor disconfirm the analysis presented in Part 2.

In addition, the analysis of Part 2 is based on a comparative statics model of the marijuana market, an economic model whose weaknesses are discussed in Chapter 4. The learning-curve model discussed elsewhere in that chapter suggests in particular that the possibility of a dichotomy between the activities of low-cost suppliers and new entrants has important consequences for the analysis of enforcement. By necessity, the predictions of Part 2 ignored these consequences; we, therefore, would not expect the analysis of Part 2 to be confirmed even if a *ceteris paribus* test were available.

That said, it remains the case that some sets of real-world consequences of the enforcement buildup would have been less consistent with our model than others. If users had begun to report widespread unavailability of marijuana starting in the mid–1980s, or if there had been a sudden upward leap in the price of marijuana of a given potency, or if consumption had taken a sharp plunge, it would be time to take our market model back to the drawing board. It is with this in mind that we investigate the effects of the Reagan years on the marijuana market.

THE EFFECTS OF THE ENFORCEMENT BUILDUP

We anticipated that an enforcement buildup would have the following effects:

Increasing enforcement-imposed costs would raise the price of the drug. While higher prices would tend to decrease consumption, the low price-elasticity of marijuana demand would keep this decrease moderate. Total dollars spent on the drug— and total dealer revenue—would therefore increase. Higher prices might also encourage substitution of other drugs for marijuana.

Intensified enforcement would be unlikely to create long-term or widespread shortages. Enforcement might, however, influence product mix, by increasing costs nonuniformly for different classes of suppliers. A program aimed at imports should boost domestic production, which is predominantly of high-potency, high-priced *sinsemilla*.

Table 10.1
Marijuana Prices, 1982–1986

		Price/oz			Price
	Low	High	G.M.*	Potency %	gram THC
1982					
Commercial	30	65	45	2.63	60.4
Sinsemilla	100	125	112	7.10	55.6
Total	40	73	55	3.26	59.5
1986					
Commercial	45	120	73	3.33	77.3
Sinsemilla	100	200	141	8.43	59.0
Total	53	133	84	4.15	71.4
1986**					
Commercial	40	106	64	3.33	67.8
Sinsemilla	88	176	124	8.43	51.9
Total	47	117	74	4.15	62.9
Change 1982–86					
Commercial	50%	84%	62%	26.6%	28%
Sinsemilla	0%	60%	26%	18.7%	6%
Total	32%	82%	53%	27.3%	20%
Change 1982–86**					
Commercial	33%	63%	42%	26.6%	12%
Sinsemilla	-12%	41%	11%	18.7%	-7%
Total	17%	60%	35%	27.3%	6%

*Geometric Mean
**Prices are adjusted for inflation of 13.6%, as reported in *Economic Report of the President* (Washington, D.C., 1987), p. 307.

Furthermore, increased enforcement would intensify the importance of violence and the threat of violence in the marijuana trade. Such violence may not be directly observable. As we have seen, enforcement may result in a reorganization of the market along more "organized," criminal lines; then threats of violence may be used by the strongest of the criminal competitors, making explicit violence unnecessary.[2]

The changes observed in the period of 1982–1986 (see tables 10.1 and 10.2) do not greatly diverge from these predictions.

Table 10.2
THC Consumption, 1982–1986

	Quantity (Tons)	Average Potency %	Net THC (Tons)
1982			
Sinsemilla	685	7.10	49
Commercial	4,210	2.63	111
Total	4,895	3.26	160
1986			
Sinsemilla	751	8.43	63
Commercial	3,945	3.33	131
Total	4,695	4.15	195
Change 1982-86			
Sinsemilla	10%	18.7%	29%
Commercial	-6%	26.6%	18%
Total	-4%	27.3%	22%

Availability and prevalence of use

1984 showed the first and only statistically significant two-year decline in marijuana availability as perceived by high school seniors; still, 85 percent think marijuana would be "very easy" or "fairly easy" to get.[3]

There do not appear to have been any prolonged or widespread shortages. The numbers of high school seniors reporting having used marijuana in the previous year and those reporting being daily users continued declines which had started in 1979.[4]

Price

NNICC estimates are given in broad price ranges; prices of commercial increased from $30–$65 per ounce to $45–$120 while prices of *sinsemilla* increased from $100–$125 to $100–$200.[5] The geometric means of the price ranges increased 42 percent for commercial and 11 percent for *sinsemilla* in constant dollars (see table 10.1). Adjusted for changes in potency (see below) commercial prices rose 6 percent and *sinsemilla* prices actually fell by 7 percent. Overall, the average price of a milligram of THC rose 6 percent, from $59 to $63.

Potency

NNICC estimates that the potency of commercial grade marijuana increased between 1982 and 1986 from 2.63 percent THC to 3.33 percent (an increase of 27 percent), while *sinsemilla* potency increased 19 percent, from 7.10 percent to 8.43 percent.[6] Furthermore, according to NNICC estimates, *sinsemilla* accounted for a growing share of the market; domestic production, largely *sinsemilla,* rose by one-fifth, from 10 percent of the total to 18 percent of the total.[7] Average potency of all marijuana consumed rose 27 percent, from 3.26 percent to 4.15 percent.

Consumption

The official estimate of total marijuana consumption (in tons) fell by 4 percent between 1982 and 1985 (no estimate was made for 1986).[8] Combined with the 27 percent increase in average potency, that implies an increase of 22 percent in actual THC consumed.

Injuries

Between 1983 and 1986 marijuana related visits to hospital emergency rooms reporting to the DAWN system rose 8 percent, from 5590 to 6046.[9] This seems to reflect the increased chance of immediate ill effects from smoking more potent marijuana, and perhaps an increased frequency of adulteration.

Substitution

It is impossible to know how much changes in alcohol and other drug consumption depend on changes in the marijuana market. However, inhalant use by high school seniors rose steadily from 1981–1986, returning to the high level of 1978 and 1980.[10]

In sum, the marijuana market responded to increased enforcement pressure as might have been anticipated: more grams of THC were packed into each ton of marijuana, and fewer tons were smuggled across the borders. In addition, domestic marijuana became less expensive relative to imported marijuana. The total number of users appears to have decreased but total potency-adjusted consumption (and injuries) rose, suggesting that there were fewer casual users, but more heavy users.

EVALUATING THE ENFORCEMENT BUILDUP

It is possible that some of the observed changes in the market were demand-driven rather than supply-driven. High school seniors, for example, report substantially less favorable attitudes toward marijuana smoking; this would help explain the decrease in the number of users without any reference to supply changes. (Though it could also be the case that as their personal and vicarious experience with marijuana shifted toward a more and more potent drug, their attitudes toward it hardened.)[11]

For the sake of analysis, we will nevertheless attribute all of the observed changes to increased enforcement. In that case, does the policy of increased enforcement count as a success or a failure?

Consumption costs

Overall consumption fell by around 4 percent; this indicates some reduction in the social costs caused by consumption. Furthermore, we have seen that the increase in potency may tend to discourage new and older users. While the behavior of older users carries few social costs, the initiation of new users can be important, since marijuana use is often an initiation into more dangerous drug habits. The number of new users increased potency discourages (by making the leap into drug use more precipitous) could be significant.

At the same time, users who continue to use marijuana are now using a more potent, and more dangerous, drug than they were previously (although some may use it less frequently). This is a significant worsening of the marijuana consumption problem. The possibility also exists that higher prices may encourage substitution of cheaper PCP, inhalants or hallucinogens for marijuana. The detrimental effect of such substitution on almost any scale would outweigh most of the other gains.

Illicit market costs

The new enforcement policy significantly reduced overseas importation. This is shown by the precipitous drop in the Colombian market share. However, much of the slack was filled by domestic and Mexican marijuana, each of which uses importation and distribution methods significantly different from those targeted by the enforcement program. We, therefore, should examine the qualitative changes that this shift produces in the costs of the illicit market.

The shift to domestic and Mexican organizations reduces the average size of a typical marijuana firm; this reduces the internal violence and increased criminality associated with large illicit enterprises. The shift to domestic markets also gives a small boost to the national economy by keeping dollars within United States borders.

No method other than speculation exists for determining whether violence and corruption were exacerbated or mitigated by increased enforcement. However, there is no reason to expect the perverse effects of increased enforcement described in Part 2 did not occur in fact. Increased enforcement against importers may reduce the chances of corruption (since it is rarer for government agents to be working alone). Violence, resulting from the market participation of more organized and criminal groups, may increase. Particularly vicious violence is also associated with domestic gardens and farms (see Chapter 7).

Evaluation

The policy of doubled marijuana enforcement begun in 1982 reduced consumption-by-weight by the order of magnitude predicted. THC consumption, however, increased dramatically, a result not predicted in our model and certainly not expected or desired by the Reagan Administration. The increase in illicit market costs are unmeasurable, but there is reason to expect that they did occur. Moreover, the shift to more potent marijuana that accompanied the new enforcement levels does have heavy social costs, especially if it is related to the increase in cocaine and inhalant use. Given this possibility, and the expenditures that the enforcement increase involved, it is hard to justify the buildup.

In addition, although dramatic costs did not result from the enforcement increase, the potential benefits of an enforcement decrease remain. Although an increase in consumption is likely, with such an increase's associated costs, substitution would be discouraged. Furthermore, low potency marijuana might again become widespread, mitigating the social costs of marijuana potency. Of course, if the shift in potency stems from a shift in consumer preferences, this would not occur.

More importantly, although the enforcement buildup did not measurably increase violence and criminality, an enforcement reduction might still be able to mitigate these features of the marijuana market. While the impact of reductions on the cnsumption costs would be mixed, this would be a clear benefit.

Finally, the possible benefits of enforcement reduction would be accompanied by significant savings for federal law enforcement.

NOTES

1. Drug Abuse Policy Office, *National and International Drug Law Enforcement Strategy (IDLES)* (Washington: National Drug Enforcement Policy Board, 1987), 187. The 1986 figures assume that the Chapter 5 calculation that 34 percent of the 1982 enforcement budget was attributable to marijuana remained relatively constant.

2. Frederick Martens, "Conflicting Goals in Narcotics Enforcement", presented at the Symposium on Organized Crime and Narcotics, Villanova University, Penn., May 9–11, 1988.

3. L. D. Johnson et al., *National Trends in Drug Use and Related Factors Among American High School Students and Young Adults, 1975–1986* (Washington: National Institute on Drug Abuse, 1987), 152.

4. Daily use was at 10.7 percent in 1979, 6.3 percent in 1982 and 4.0 percent in 1982. Johnston, *National Trends in Drug Use,* 48–50.

5. National Narcotics Intelligence Consumers Committee, *Narcotics Intelligence Estimate 1987* (Washington: Drug Enforcement Administration, 1988), 9.

6. Mahmoud El Sohly, *Potency Monitor Project* (University, Miss.: Research Institute of Pharmaceutical Sciences, 1988), 4, table 2, and *Narcotics Intelligence Estimate 1985–1986* (Washington: National Narcotics Intelligence Consumers Committee, 1987), 8. The trend has been towards more potent marijuana for the better part of a decade, and anecdotal evidence would lead one to believe that the increase is even greater than NNICC's estimate. Since NNICC's potency estimates are based on analysis of whatever the DEA chanced to seize they are considered somewhat unreliable; it is in fact likely that the actual increase is considerbly higher.

7. NNICC, *Narcotics Intelligence Estimate 1987,* 18–19.

8. From 4,899 metric tons to 4,693 metric tons. NNICC, *Narcotics Intelligence Estimate 1985–1986,* 6. The 1985 figure is the estimate used in Chapter 3 to approximate the consumption in 1986; similarly, we will use four percent as the decrease between 1982–1986.

9. National Institute on Drug Abuse, *Annual Data 1983: Data from the Drug Abuse Warning Network (DAWN)* (Washington: Drug Enforcement Administration, 1984), 22 and *Annual Data 1986,* 26.

10. Johnston, *National Trends in Drug Use,* 49.

11. Peter Reuter has suggested that these decreases may also be related to a concurrent decline in the social acceptability of smoking of any kind, stemming from changes in attitude towards cigarette smoking.

11

The Question of Legalization

If less enforcement is better, wouldn't no enforcement be best? Doesn't the argument of this book point logically to the legalization of marijuana?[1] Not necessarily.

The argument presented so far does not depend on any specific evaluation of the dangers of marijuana as an abusable drug. If, as we have argued, federal marijuana enforcement influences the extent of marijuana consumption only negligibly, while worsening the effects on users of the remaining consumption and increasing the wealth and power of criminal organizations and their use of violence and corruption, then federal marijuana enforcement ought to be cut back. When a program has obvious costs and no substantial benefits, complicated questions of relative valuation are almost irrelevant.

But legalization is more than the logical extension of a policy of decreased enforcement. Consumption patterns for legally available marijuana might be utterly unlike those for illegal marijuana, even if that illegality is only weakly supported by enforcement. A judgment about legalization rests on two hard questions, one empirical and one evaluative. Empirically, we need to ask by how much legalization would increase consumption, and what sorts of users the increased consumption would involve. On an evaluative level, we need to ask how bad (or, conceivably, good)[2] that increase would be. Nothing said above implies a clear answer to either question.

This chapter will attempt a sketch—no more than that—of how the analysis of legalization, and of the related but quite distinct question of decriminalization, might proceed. The reader is warned that it reaches no conclusion; unlike the question, "Should we cut back on federal marijuana enforcement?" the question, "Should we legalize marijuana?" does not have an obviously correct answer.

Legalization would largely eliminate black-market costs in illicit revenues, enforcement expenditure, violence and corruption. It might even yield substantial revenues for the government. Against these benefits would be the costs that would flow from the increase it would likely create in consumption levels. If legalization led to a consumption increase of 10 percent above current levels it would have to be counted as a good move. If legalization led instead to a tripling of use—particularly in the number of very heavy users—any but the most sanguine about the drug's effects would probably count legalization as a disaster. Such a disaster would be hard to reverse, since an expanded user population could multiply enforcement problems. The problem for the analyst is that a 10 percent increase and a tripling seem equally plausible outcomes of legalization.

The question whether marijuana ought to be legally available for "recreational" use is entangled with the question whether it has therapeutic value for specific diseases and ought to be available for physicians to prescribe. That entanglement is unnecessary. Alcohol and nicotine are no longer used medically but are legally available for recreational use; cocaine and the barbiturates are used as medicine but taboo outside the therapeutic context. However, as the therapeutic-uses debate is important in its own right and is always raised as an issue in the legalization debate, it may be as well to get that argument out of the way first.

MEDICAL USES

Marijuana, THC, and various derivatives or synthetic analogues have been used or proposed for use for a variety of medical purposes: to counteract the nausea that accompanies chemotherapy in cancer treatment, to reduce intraocular pres-

sure for glaucoma victims, to control the spasticity characteristic of multiple sclerosis and sometimes found in paraplegia
and quadraplegia, and to treat chronic pain from a variety of
underlying diseases.[3] The question of cannabis therapeutics
has been tied up in more than a decade of courtroom and regulatory proceedings. These proceedings involve two linked
questions. The Drug Enforcement Administration under power
delegated by the Attorney General pursuant to the Controlled
Substances Act, must decide whether marijuana is to remain
in Schedule I, which means that it is contraband except for the
most limited research purposes, or should be moved to Schedule
II or Schedule III, either of which would make it available by
prescription. The legal question is whether marijuana has any
"recognized medical use" (in which case it should be resched-
uled) or not (in which case it should remain in Schedule I). A
petition for rescheduling filed in 1986 by a coalition called the
Alliance for Cannabis Therapeutics (ACT) has been twice denied by the administration and twice sent back for rehearing
by the courts.[4] As of this writing, a third hearing has resulted
in an administrative decision in favor of removing marijuana
from Schedule I and rescheduling it in Schedule II.[5]

A parallel process involves the Food and Drug Administration, which must decide whether marijuana, its active principles, or their analogues should be approved for use as drugs.
This question is linked to the DEA scheduling process in two
ways. Opponents of rescheduling argue that a drug cannot have
a "recognized medical use" if the FDA has never approved it.
However, while a drug remains contraband it is very difficult
to carry out the human clinical trials on which new drug approval would be based.

While the DEA has approved THC and synthetic derivatives
for medical use, it has yet to approve the use of the unprocessed
plant. The reasons for this schism are largely professional,
bureaucratic and political, rather than medical. THC and synthetic derivatives are pure chemical species, taken orally, as
opposed to marijuana, a mixture of psychoactives which is in-
haled. Good medicine and good regulation, as the FDA under-
stands them, depend on careful dosage and controlled double-
blind studies.[6] Because subjects differ in the way they smoke,

and because marijuana is not a pure chemical species but contains a mix of psychoactive principles which varies from plant to plant and even from one part to another of the same plant, it is virtually impossible to administer a controlled dosage or to repeat that dosage from subject to subject. This immensely complicates the clinical trial process, already complicated enough due to marijuana's current contraband status and the unavailability of patent protection for a drug manufacturer who did succeed in obtaining FDA approval.

More fundamentally, telling a patient to smoke the leaves and flowers of a plant seems to have more in common with folk medicine than with "real" medicine, which gives known dosages of known compounds in the form of a pill or injection. The physician exercises less control over dosage than in the classical prescription form (e.g., "Two tablets every four hours"); the process of administration is simply out of step with modern medical practice. Add to this the antismoking campaign and the association of marijuana with illicit intoxication, and the regulatory outcome is easy to understand.

But to understand the outcome is not to approve it. Marijuana appears to have some substantial advantages over THC, and smoking over oral dosage, for several of the medical situations under consideration.

THC appears to engender *more* unpleasant side effects, particularly psychoactive ones, than marijuana itself.[7] Precisely why is unknown; perhaps some of the other active principles in marijuana act as dampers.

Smoking has obvious advantages over swallowing a pill where the goal is controlling nausea. Moreover, the time lag from swallowing a pill to getting its effects is long and variable. The medicine must be absorbed into the bloodstream before it sets to work, and how long that takes will depend on a variety of factors, particularly whether the stomach is full or empty. By contrast, a drug taken in through the lung hits the bloodstream almost immediately. This allows the patient to "titrate" the dosage, taking a little at a time until the desired relief is obtained. No such titration is possible for oral doses. Thus smoking, while it reduces the physician's control over dosage, potentially increases the patient's.

To set against these advantages, smoking has equally obvious disadvantages. Inhaling hot gasses and particulates is
bad for the throat and lung. In addition, marijuana smoke has
substantial concentrations of carbon monoxide and of carcinogenic "coal tars." Both the experiments in the literature and
the ongoing quasi-legal therapeutic uses of marijuana seem to
involve smoking "joints." It is unclear why water pipes, which
cool the hot gasses and filter out particulates and coal tars
without absorbing THC or the other active principles, are not
considered or used.

The hearing record seems to amply bear out the claim that
marijuana does have a range of medical uses not matched by
its derivatives.[8] The remaining argument against down-sched-
uling is that permitting the medical use of marijuana would
increase its illicit use. But marijuana is already so widely available illicitly that "leakage" from any legal supply seems unlikely to make any substantial difference, any more than the
legal cocaine used in dentistry and ophthalmic surgery is an
important source of the supply of that drug for illicit purposes.
Nor does the fact that cocaine is a Schedule II drug rather than
a Schedule I drug appear to have played any role in determining public attitudes toward it.

Thus the medical-uses debate over marijuana can safely be
decided on its medical merits, without any serious consideration of its effects on unsupervised use. If that decision were
made on its medical merits, the record so far suggests that
marijuana would be allowed to reenter the licit pharmacopeia.
While some of the proponents, and many of the opponents, of
"cannabis therapeutics" clearly regard the recognition of medical use as the entering wedge for full legalization, their hopes
and fears alike seem unfounded.

The argument for legal medical use is thus completely separate from the debate over the various enforcement options.
One can enforce the current prohibition with as much or as
little force as one wants irrespective of its medical status.
The introduction of the argument over the medical use of
marijuana into the debate over enforcement is politically mo-
tivated; they ought instead to be treated as two distinct issues.

LEGALIZATION

Whether or not marijuana is to be used medically, there remains the question of whether it should be legally available for nonmedical, "recreational" use. This is far from being a simple yes-or-no question. Those who favor legalization face a number of subordinate questions: Legal for whom? At what price? Under what conditions? That is to say, they face the problem of designing a regulatory regime and thinking through how such a regime could be administered. Once such a regime is designed, one can proceed to the questions of what its advantages and disadvantages might be when compared to the current position.

Designing a Regulatory Regime

Imagine that all references to marijuana were removed from the statute books, leaving it legal as bread and baling wire are legal: taxed only as other items subject to sales tax, sold without any health warnings, available for sale in unlimited quantities to anyone with money (including children), freely avertised in all media. That would make it far more legal—far less regulated and discouraged—than alcoholic beverages or tobacco. A thoroughgoing libertarian would presumably support such a policy, but others, even supporters of "legalization" in some sense, would have doubts.

The concerns that led to the prohibition of marijuana—concerns about abuse, about misconduct under the influence, above all about damage to children—would not disappear with marijuana prohibition. A variety of restrictions might be placed on the drug in an attempt to limit the harms tht might come from its increased availability. A partial list might include forbidding sale to minors; restricting sale to licensed vendors; placing limits on the places and times of sale; limiting advertising with respect either to content or media; requiring health warnings on packages, in advertising, or at the point of sale; and restricting potency and/or quantity. Legal marijuana would also be a candidate for heavy taxation, both to restrict consumption and to raise revenue.[9]

Any regulation creates the possibility of violation. Wherever there are tariffs, there are smugglers. Regulation, like prohibition, would need to be enforced. The more restrictive the regulation, the stronger the motivation for ignoring or evading it. Thus, a regulatory regime, like prohibition, may create illicit-market costs.

Taxation

Untaxed licit marijuana would be very cheap. As a slightly processed agricultural product, bulk marijuana resembles pipe tobacco and tea, both of which are quoted in dollars per pound rather than tens of dollars per ounce. Very heavy specific excise taxation would therefore be necessary to keep licit marijuana from falling enormously in price.

That marijuana demand is relatively insensitive to small variations around its current price does not imply that very dramatic price decreases would not produce correspondingly large consumption-volume increases. In addition, the demand for legally available marijuana may be more responsive to price changes than is the demand for prohibited marijuana, because consumers will not face the nondollar costs of black market purchase and consumption and thus dollar price will loom larger in their purchase and use decisions.

In addition to avoiding a potentially explosive increase in consumption, heavy marijuana taxation could be a substantial revenue raiser. Since licit marijuana would be cheap to produce and market, a large slice of the current $14 billion in annual illicit marijuana revenues would be available as potential tax revenues even if legalization did not itself increase consumption levels. Any such increase would further swell the potential tax take. Restriction of legal availability to adults would tend to decrease tax revenues.

On the other hand, heavy taxation would encourge untaxed production: "moonshining." This could involve either strictly illicit domestic production or import, or simply diversion of product from licit channels before tax was paid. To control such moonshining, there would need to be a class of "revenooers," or tax enforcers. This situation would tend to reproduce the illicit-markets problems of the current regime, though on a smaller scale, as moonshiners used violence and corruption to maintain their traffic. At current black market prices, marijuana has a far higher ratio of value to bulk than, for instance, untaxed tobacco or alcohol. That fact would facilitate moonshining. Maintaining vigorous revenue enforcement might prove difficult; agents may be more willing to work hard and take risks if their mission is to suppress the availability of a dangerous drug than if it is to support the revenue collection process.[10]

Lower levels of taxation would discourage "moonshining" by reducing its potential rewards, and consequently reduce black market violence and corruption and the difficulty of revenue enforcement. On the other hand, they would yield smaller amounts of revenue and higher consumption levels. The choice between high and low taxation under a legal regime resembles the choice between legalization and continued prohibition: a trade-off between illicit-market costs and the harms of increased consumption.

Restrictions on users

The most obvious restriction to place on legal marijuana use is the prohibition of use by minors. Since minors currently account for a significant percentage of marijuana consumption,[11] the imposition of a relatively late "smoking age" (between 18 and 21, similar to the drinking age for alcohol) would thus leave much of current marijuana consumption illegal. This might support a continued black market. If the existing enforcement machinery were left in place, this smaller market (with older users drained off by the licit supply) might find it hard to function; marijuana from illicit sources might be less available to kids than it is today. In addition, poor kids who finance their marijuana consumption from the proceeds of illicit marijuana sales might find themselves cut off. But, as with alcohol, one would have to expect significant leakage from the (licit) adult market into the (illicit) juvenile one, with older siblings or friends supplying younger ones. Also as with alcohol, the enforcement and social sanctions against illicit juvenile use of a legal drug would probably be significantly less grave and less severely enforced than those against the use of an illegal drug. On balance, then, age restrictions within a regulatory regime would probably leave marijuana more available to minors than it is now.

Restrictions on Potency and Quantity

Black market marijuana currently varies enormously in its THC content. Consumers are only imperfectly informed about those variations. A regulatory regime could include measurement and labelling. It could also include an upper limit on potency, on the theory that more potent mixtures are more likely to lead to intense or unexpected levels of intoxication.

Neither potency labelling nor potency restriction would directly address the problem of very heavy users. That problem could be addressed in part by limiting the total quantity any individual could purchase during a given month or year. Such a limit would have to be enforced by keeping a central register of purchases (the system might resemble the one currently used to verify credit card purchases). It is easy to imagine complications and evasions (purchases made in another state, purchases by proxy) and regulatory enforcement efforts. Considered in advance, the whole scheme may seem hopelessly artificial and baroque, a regulatory Rube Goldberg device. But if legalization were to greatly increase the number of "marijuanaholics," the benefits of quantity restriction might be seen to outweigh its costs.

Restrictions on Time and Place of Use

A regulatory regime would prohibit or restrict the purchase of marijuana at times and places where it is most in danger of abuse. State monopolies on sales, as exist for alcohol, might be instituted. Other possible restrictions include bans on use in public places and the licensing or prohibition of "coffeehouses" supplying marijuana by the joint or pipe for consumption on the premises.

Restrictions on Marketing and Advertising

To allow a licit market to develop to meet an exiting demand is one thing; to allow participants in that market to create additional demand is another. The relentless promotion by state lottery commissions of the virtues of gambling at very poor odds are a warning of the ease with which a vice goes from being prohibited to being promoted when revenue is at stake.

Marijuana advertising might be prohibited entirely. Proposed restrictions on tobacco advertising have met with opposition on First Amendment grounds, though it is difficult for a nonlawyer to understand why Congress can ban a product altogether but not permit its production and forbid its promotion. A more serious objection would be that the absence of advertised price competition would facilitate tacit collusion among producers to raise prices. This could be remedied by permitting advertisements giving only the name, price, and potency of the product and the address of the seller, after the fashion of the "tombstone" advertisements for new securities (also the product of regulation).

An alternative to any restriction on advertising would be the requirement of equal time (or space) for "negative" advertising, as was the case with television tobacco ads before they were banned. Similarly, advertisements might be required to carry warnings, as might packages.

But designing such restrictions in advance is one thing, and keeping them in force is another. Legalization, unless in the form of a government monopoly, would create an industry with strong interests in promoting sales. Legalization in the form of a government monopoly would create a direct state interest in promoting sales. In either case, regulators and legislators would face pressures similar in kind if not in force to the ones around alcohol and tobacco regulation.

Sanctions against Reckless Behavior under the Influence

The harm done by marijuana use to driving behavior and productivity on the job is subject to some debate; nevertheless, sanctions against marijuana intoxication on the job or while driving seem likely components of the regulatory regime. However, as in the case of alcohol, it may become difficult to regulate drug-related behavior where the drug's consumption is well established. Judges and juries in drunk driving cases are often lenient to defendants who, after all, only had a few drinks.

Enforcement against inappropriate marijuana intoxication is even more difficult than that for alcohol intoxication since there is no convenient "breathalyzer" test for marijuana. Urine tests can pick up the presence of THC in the blood, but this is a measure of past drug use, not current dosage, and may not reflect accurately the level of drug influence because of tolerance and other variables. A useful test would need to be physiological or psychometric rather than chemical. These testing difficulties would make enforcement especially difficult, even more difficult than enforcement against inappropriate alcohol intoxication, which is thought by many peole to be inadequate. The development of a cheap, reliable test for marijuana intoxication would be a major hurdle for a regulatory regime.

Costs and Benefits of Legalization

Legalization would reduce the harms done by illicit markets and the costs of enforcement while converting several billions of dollars per year of criminals' incomes into government revenue. This last point is treated as a throwaway line by the proponents of legalization and as a mere debating point by its opponents, but if those revenues were used for heroin enforcement and anti–drug abuse educational programs, the net effect might be less crime *and* less drug abuse. If the foregone revenues are thought of as an "opportunity cost" of prohibition— as they surely should be—it is far from clear that prohibition is worth $10 billion per year.[12]

Moreover, legalization would create clear benefits for consumers who did not increase their marijuana consumption and for those whose increased consumption did them no net harm. They would find themselves once again on the right side of the law and at reduced risk of buying and using adulterated drugs. Some might benefit by substituting marijuana for other licit or illicit drugs. In addition, the legalization of marijuana might make drug education more effective, thus reducing the amount of other drugs consumed. Marijuana is smoked by millions of teenagers with no marked short-term effect. Legally classing this drug, which is perceived to be relatively benign, with drugs such as cocaine and PCP, undermines drug education efforts; if students see part of the message as untrue or at least exaggerated, then they are less apt to believe the rest.

Against all this are the great unknowns: the increase in consumption, and particuarly in the number of very heavy users.

Illegality, independent of the degree of enforcement, forces on an illicit market a different capital structure, a different marketing and distribution system, and a different set of employment relationships from those encountered for licit goods. Peter Reuter has called these differences the "structural consequences of product illegality."[13] These differences mean that information travels much more slowly from one participant to another and that agreements between them are not legally enforceable. The result is higher prices, less reliable quality, and greater variability of supply across consumers and over time.[14] Moreover, for some consumers all of the time and for all consumers at some times, illegality is a deterrent to consumption even if the risk of arrest is small.[15]

The history of alcohol prohibition and its repeal suggests that changes in a drug's legal status, even if the drug is already widely consumed and even if enforcement is far from perfect, can substantially change the number of very heavy users. Not only did estimates of total alcohol consumed fall substantially when the Eighteenth Amendment was enacted and rise substantially after its repeal, but deaths from cirrhosis of the liver—a sensitive indicator of current heavy consumption by chronic heavy users—kept pace; cirrhosis deaths fell by a factor of three between 1918 and 1921, and began to climb again by 1935, two years after repeal.[16]

Such an increase in very heavy marijuana usage after legalization would likely lead to demands for its reprohibition. But such a step would not restore the status quo ante. If legalization were to greatly increase the size of the marijuana market, the illicit-market harms under a fresh prohibition would be proportionately greater. Some of those introduced to marijuana use during a period of legality would abstain again once prohibition returned; the remainder would swell the revenues of illicit marijuana dealers and multiply the headaches of marijuana enforcement agents.

Thus legalization, while it would almost certainly have great benefits, might well have even greater costs, and could not be easily or cheaply reversed if it proved a mistake. The policy would be very difficult to reverse. Not only would the existence of a licit industry, the source of employment and tax revenues, pose substantial political problems, but the recriminalization of the drug would leave the country in a much worse position than it now is with respect to marijuana enforcement. The increased number of users would create a larger market base for the newly illegal industry, thus increasing the size of the enforcement effort necessary to control it and the illicit-market spinoff crime and inequities it would create.

DECRIMINALIZATION

Decriminalization—treating marijuana consumption and possession for private use as either legal or only mildly punishable while leaving its distribution a criminal offense—is often viewed as a middle ground between prohibition and legalization. This is a mistake. Decriminalization deserves to be considered as a distinct policy, with its own characteristic problems and advantages.

Decriminalization would leave marijuana in much the same legal position as alcohol held during Prohibition: legal to have and use but not to sell. As such, it would carry costs different from both legalization and total prohibition in three important areas: enforcement expenditure, consumption, and the illicit market.

Arrests

By reducing arrests made, decriminalization, like legalization, would save enforcement resources. About 300,000 arrests for marijuana possession were made in 1986;[17] eliminating these would relieve some strain from an overworked enforcement system and save on processing costs.

In addition, decriminalization, like legalization, would reduce the tension between otherwise law-abiding marijuana smokers and the law enforcement system and the damage done to users by arrest and criminal justice processing. The tension between the deterrent value of stiff sanctions and the interests of those being punished pervades the criminal justice system, but never so painfully as when the purpose of the prohibition is precisely to protect those who otherwise might engage in the behavior prohibited. If a prison term for robbery damages the robber—even makes him a worse citizen in the long run—it may still protect robbery victims. But there is a limit to how much damage one would want to do to marijuana smokers to prevent them from damaging themselves. (Here the question of "user sanctions" can be seen as the flip side of the decriminalization debate; decriminalization risks additional consumption in order to spare the damage to users while user sanctions increase the potential damage in order to reduce consumption. The ideal would be to find sanctions with a high ratio of current unpleasantness—and therefore deterrent value—to long-range damage.)

Consumption

Under decriminalization, despite the absence of sanctions against possession, marijuana would still not be freely purchasable and would remain subject to variations in supply and quality. Surveys do not suggest that fear of arrest plays any substantial role in discouraging marijuana use. The inference that decriminalization would increase consumption only slightly seems to be borne out by the results of the decriminalization of use in various states in the mid–1970s: no evidence of increased consumption in the states has emerged. This fact led a National Academy of Sciences panel to recommend decriminalization.[18]

On the other hand, it is difficult to guess the long-term effects of national decriminalization. If marijuana had been decriminalized nationally in the 1970s, would attitudes about it have hardened as much as they did in the subsequent decade?[19] These attitudinal changes do seem to be connected with decreased self-reported consumption.

Illicit Market

Even if decriminalization increases consumption only slightly, it is a worse policy from the illicit-market perspective than either legalization or the continued prohibition of use as well as sale. By (possibly) increasing consumption of a drug whose production and distribution remain in entirely illicit hands, decriminalization benefits sellers. At the same time, sellers remain unthreatened by free competition and government regulation. A rational marijuana trafficker ought to fear legalization above all things, but he should regard decriminalization as an entirely good idea.

CONCLUSION

Reducing federal marijuana enforcement is as close to betting on a sure thing as any real-world decision is likely to be. Legalization is a heavy wager on a coin flip. Decriminalization saves enforcement costs and avoids criminalizing a widespread activity, but may lead to increased consumption in the long run and tends to worsen the illicit market problems. Neither the choice between continued prohibition and legalization nor the decision whether to spare the users while going after the traffickers can be made on purely analytic grounds.

NOTES

1. After almost a decade of being scarcely mentioned, legalization has returned as a topic of public and scholarly discussion. Cf. Ethan Nadelmann, "The Case for Legalization," and Harry Kaplan, "Taking Drugs Seriously," *The Public Interest* 92 (Summer 1988): 3–50; Kurt L. Schmoke in an article by Peter Kerr, "The Unspeakable is Debated: Should Drugs be Legalized?" *New York Times* 15 May 1988: A1; and *The Regulation and Taxation of Cannabis Commerce* (National Task Force on Cannabis Regulation, December 1982).

2. Cf. Michael Kinsley, "Glass Houses and Getting Stoned," *Time*, 6 June 1988, 92.

3. R. C. Randall, ed., *Marijuana, Medicine and the Law* (Washington: Galen Press, 1988).

4. Randall, *Marijuana, Medicine and the Law.*

5. Francis L. Young, *Opinion and Recommended Ruling, Findings of Fact, Conclusions of Law and Decision of Administrative Law Judge in the Matter of Marijuana Rescheduling Petition,* United States Department of Justice, Drug Enforcement Administration, Docket no. 86–22, 6 September 1988, 67–68.

6. Daniel Dansak, "Affidavit of Daniel Dansak, M. D.," ed. Randall, *Marijuana, Medicine and the Law,* 128.

7. Deborah Goldberg, "Affidavit of Deborah Baron Goldberg, M. D.," ed. Randall, *Marijuana, Medicine and the Law,* 160 and 186.

8. Young, *Opinion and Recommended Ruling.*

9. Details of possible legalization schemes are discussed in Klaus Kolb, "The Legalization of Marijuana," (unpublished paper, Policy Analysis Exercise, Kennedy School of Government, Harvard University, June 1984). Kolb argues strongly that legalization would be, on balance, beneficial.

10. This point was raised by Thomas C. Schelling.

11. The twelve to seventeen age group made up 15 percent of the current smokers in 1985. National Institute on Drug Abuse, *National Household Survey on Drug Abuse: Population Estimates 1985* (Washington: Department of Health and Human Services, 1987), 10.

12. The author made a rather tongue-in-cheek argument along these lines some years ago. Cf. "Marijuana Prohibition Doesn't Pass Gramm-Rudman Test," *Wall Street Journal,* 8 May 1986, 30.

13. Peter Reuter, *Disorganized Crime: The Economics of the Visible Hand* (Cambridge, Mass.: MIT Press, 1983), 109ff.

14. Reuter, *Disorganized Crime,* 113–123.

15. Risk of arrest for possession is 2 percent per user-year in 1982. J. Michael Polich et al., *Strategies for Controlling Adolescent Drug Use* (Santa Monica, Cal.: RAND Corporation, 1984), 58.

16. Total consumption was returning to the 1915 level by 1945. See Dean Gerstein, "Alcohol Use and Consequences," in Mark Moore and Dean Gerstein, eds., *Alcohol and Public Policy: Beyond the Shadow of Prohibition* (Washington: National Academy Press, 1981), 195.

17. Federal Bureau of Investigation, *Uniform Crime Reports: Crime in the United States, 1986* (Washington: Department of Justice, 1987), 163–64.

18. L. D. Johnston et al., *National Trends in Drug Use, and Related Factors among American High School Students and Young Adults, 1975–1986* (Washington: National Institute on Drug Abuse, 1987), 131.

19. Johnston quoted in *An Analysis of Marijuana Policy,* Commission on Behavioral and Social Sciences and Education, (Washington: National Academy Press, 1982), 14 and 244.

12

A Marijuana Policy Recommendation

It is no longer 1982, but 1986, and you are once again drug advisor to the administration. Four years of the Reagan enforcement buildup are behind you, but the war on drugs has not yet been won.

The marijuana market has changed since 1982. Consumption has dropped slightly, but users are smoking a more potent, dangerous product. Some users may have also substituted other, more dangerous drugs for marijuana. The illicit market has changed as well: importation from Colombia and other overseas countries is down, but Mexican and domestic production are both up. Methods and violence peculiar to overland importation as opposed to sea trade have appeared.

Despite these changes, both the marijuana business and governmental efforts against it remain essentially unchanged since 1982. Marijuana can still be grown inexpensively almost anywhere, and neither its cultivation nor its distribution requires special skills; therefore, shortages are difficult to create. Demand for the drug is still high and inelastic about its current price, which makes marijuana use only feebly responsive to increased enforcement; therefore, it is unlikely that dramatic cuts in consumption can be attained. The details of the analysis of Part 2 are complicated by the developments of the eighties, in particular by the substitution of domestic *sinsemilla* for foreign commercial varieties, but in its outlines the argument remains essentially the same.

The central question also remains: given these facts, including the fact of a four-year enforcement buldup, what is the wisest course for the government to take?

Three basic policy alternatives exist at the close of 1986. The government could legalize marijuana; it could maintain or even increase marijuana enforcement levels; or it could drastically reduce enforcement levels, along the lines suggested in Part 2.

We noted in the introduction that the choice of marijuana policy depends on both empirical and evaluative claims. A decision depends first on analyzing how the consumption and illicit market problems will respond to any given policy; then the set of effects of each policy should be compared and the most desirable one selected.

The summary below evaluates each major policy alternative in light of this dichotomy, using the analysis of the previous chapters.

Legalization

The developments of the eighties do not significantly change our analysis of marijuana legalization. Legalization is a radical, near-complete solution to the problem of the illicit marijuana market, but risks a potentially huge increase in the social costs of consumption.

Legalization would mean the end of the illicit industry and the opportunity for marijuana taxation and regulation. It is also likely to lead to an explosion in the number of users. This increase in consumption could be reversed only with great difficulty and at high cost.

Proponents of legalization claim that the illicit market does much more harm than consumption. We have seen in chapter 1 that there is no consensus about the costs of marijuana consumption; adoption of legalization would assume that these costs were relatively low. If this is a misassessment, and the costs are in fact great, legalization would have greatly worsened the marijuana problem, and its damage would be difficult to undo.

In short, the argument for legalization is founded on value

judgments about which there is no consensus rather than on analysis. It is a policy of great potential benefits but also of high risks.

Maintenance or Increase of High Enforcement Levels

Part 2 suggested that raising levels would reduce consumption only slightly while significantly worsening the illicit-market problem. This position was based on the low elasticity of demand for marijuana and the ease of its production.

The results of the policy of high enforcement adopted in the early eighties allow us to evaluate and to refine this analysis. Consumption decreased somewhat, by about 4 percent, during the period of high enforcement. Furthermore, part of the decrease seems to be among new users, a group we have noted as being of special concern. We also expect that high enforcement worsened the illicit market problem, but illicit market costs are not directly quantifiable; the market problem probably did get worse, but not enough for substantial costs to be appreciated and measured by society at large.

The other major cost of the increased enforcement policy, not predicted by analysis, appears to have been an increase in the harm done to marijuana and ex-marijuana users. Those users who quit under high enforcement are better off than they were before; but those users who continued are significantly worse off. The increase in both the price and potency of marijuana and the possible substitution of very dangerous and inexpensive drugs all seem to mitigate the benefits of a reduction in the overall number of users. Increased enforcement leaves us with a smaller, but tougher, drug problem.

Increased enforcement had equivocal results in the area of consumption even as it worsened the illicit-market problem somewhat. Representing a substantial dedication of resources, the policy of increased enforcement does not seem to have produced benefits in line with its costs.

Analysis of increased enforcement also has an evaluative component. In recommending against high enforcement, we claim that the harm done by marijuana consumption is not absolute, and that the reduction in consumption that increased enforcement brings can be mitigated by other costs. Reducing consumption, while a good, is not the only good. Although evaluative, this is not a radical view. Medical and behavioral evidence do not at all suggest that the costs of marijuana consumption are so high as to warrant very high costs elsewhere.

However, our evaluation of increased enforcement does not depend only on an evaluative claim. It also rests on the analytic conclusion: that the government is not able to reduce consumption without imposing other, significant costs on users and on society. It costs society too much, in monetary, illicit-market, and drug abuse terms, to make potential reductions in marijuana consumption worthwhile.

Enforcement Reduction

The policy of increased enforcement cannot be said to have done significant damage to the country's drug problem. Neither does it represent clear progress. Despite the differences between 1982 and 1986, we suggest that the policy analyzed in depth in Part 2—a severe enforcement cutback—remains the best alternative for dealing with the nation's marijuana problem. This is because the basic nature of the 1982 market—a consumption problem relatively insensitive to enforcement combined with an illicit-market problem that worsens as enforcement increases—holds true of the 1986 market as well.

The cost of federal marijuana enforcement in 1986 was $636 million, with $473 million for investigations, $21 million for prosecutions, and $78 million for incarceration.[1] This is 50 percent more than the cost in 1982 in current dollars, or a third more in real, constant dollars. In return, enforcement has imposed costs of $1.1 billion on the marijuana market, one-third more than in 1982 in current dollars, or 20 percent more in constant dollars.[2] Meanwhile, the marijuana industry has grown. Both the imported and domestic marijuana markets grew by 50 percent, from a total of $9.4 billion to $14 billion.[3] Enforcement-imposed costs are thus still only 11 percent of the retail imported market.

The impact of reduced drug enforcement on the consumption problem is complex. It would reduce substitution of other drugs, making those users apt to switch from marijuana to harder drugs better off; but it would harm other users by allowing them to obtain marijuana more cheaply and easily. The extent of this harm is likely to be small, however. If the enforcement budget was cut in half, to $320 million (3 percent of the market for imported marijuana), price would decrease by about 3.5 percent.[4] Quantity consumed would therefore go up only approximately 1.5 percent using the − .4 price-elasticity estimate.

An enforcement cutback's effect on the illicit-market problem might also be dramatic. By making growing and importation less dangerous, thereby lowering the price of an inelastically demanded product, it would decrease criminal revenue. It would also take away the competitive advantage enjoyed by criminals skilled in violence and corruption, reducing these and marijuana-associated crimes. If one halved the marijuana enforcement budget, criminal revenue would decrease 2 percent, while the budget of marijuana smokers would increase by the same amount.

An overall evaluation of the impact of reduction on harm done by enforcement depends on whether the shift to potent marijuana seen in the 1980s was demand- or supply-based (see chapter 10). As we have seen, the tastes of heavy users, not increased enforcement, may have been the determining factor of the shift to dangerous, more potent marijuana. If this is so, enforcement reduction is a less attractive policy than it was in 1982, since one of its effects—increased marijuana consumption—is more grave in 1986 than 1982. Other benefits of the policy, including a decrease in substitution of other drugs, remain.

If, however, the shift to potent marijuana was related to the new enforcement levels, enforcement reduction gains an additional advantage: the consumption increases it would bring about ought to be accompanied by a potency decrease. Therefore, although we would expect consumption figures to rise from the lower 1986 levels to above 1982 levels, the damage done by consumption would rise in not nearly as great a ratio.

Reduced enforcement has the potential to lower the social

costs of the illicit market below their 1982 levels. At the same time, the changes it might cause in consumption patterns might leave society with a consumption problem not significantly worse than that of 1986. Even if the shift to potent marijuana was demand based, the consumption costs should not be unbearably high; and enforcement reduction, unlike legalization, does not share the problem of irreversibility.

The recommendation of this book—to significantly reduce federal marijuana enforcement levels—depends, as does any policy recommendation, on an evaluative claim. To accept it, one must agree that the illicit market does harm society and that the damage marijuana consumption does is not so grave as to make trade-offs unworthy of consideration. I believe that this judgment is supported in both its clauses by available data and by medical and behavioral studies.

Beyond this judgment, however, the argument for reduced enforcement is insensitive to a broad range of factual and evaluative disagreements. All the calculations of previous chapters have been more conservative than necessary, and they still suggest that the ability of the government to deter consumption is severely limited. Thus, one might believe that our price and consumption estimates are off by a factor of two that marijuana does a lot of damage or that it damages only its heaviest users; that its use is a vice immoral in itself or a civil liberty unfairly denied American citizens in the name of the few it harms; that it is a gateway to social problems or a helpful preventative; and still be convinced that reducing enforcement to a low but visible level is the best way to minimize the costs that marijuana imposes on the nation.

NOTES

1. These figures were arrived at using the assumptions and methods detailed fully in chapter 5. The budget numbers all came from *National and International Drug Law Enforcement Strategy* (Washington: National Drug Enforcement Policy Board, 1987), 182–187. The percentage of DEA work hours spent on marijuana came from the *Annual Statistical Report 1986* (Washington: Drug Enforcement Administration, 1987). The OCDE-TF marijuana convictions came

from OCDE-TF *Annual Report of the Organized Crime Drug Enforcement Task Force Program 1986* (Washington: Department of Justice, 1987). The percentage of time devoted to marijuana by the Coast Guard came from the percentage of arrests due to marijuana made by the Coast Guard, from *United States Coast Guard Law Enforcement Digest of Interdiction Statistics* (Washington: Coast Guard, June 1988). The percentage of marijuana convictions made by the DEA was from *Federal Drug Enforcement Progress Report 1986* (Washington: National Drug Policy Board, 1987), 39. The number of prison years of accrual was calculated using numbers of convictions and length of average sentence from the DEA Defendant Statistical System. The estimate of the cost of a year in prison came from the number of prisoners, 41, 512, *Annual Statistical Report,* (Washington: Bureau of Prisons, 1987), table A–1, divided into the budget, $627.5 million, *Budget of the United States Government Fiscal Year 1988* (Washington: U.S. Office of Management and Budget, 1988), 4–127.

2. These figures were arrived at using the assumptions and methods detailed fully in chapter 5. The volume of seizures, 1,300 metric tons, was estimated from the Federal Wide Drug Seizure System, DEA Statistical Services Section. This estimate was for 1987, and was about half of the total reported seizures for Customs, Coast Guard, DEA, FBI, and the INS. The figure 1,300 metric tons is one-half of the total reported seizures for 1986, National Drug Policy Board, *Federal Drug Enforcement,* 44, 76. Assets seized, $212 million, came from the *Annual Statistical Report 1986*. The years of prison accrual came from the DEA Defendant Statistical System.

3. These figures are derived in chapter 3.

4. This is using the 1/12 ratio of imposed costs to price increase explained in chapter 6. In this case the reverse of this calculation is used for price decrease.

Bibliography

Administrative Office of the U.S. Courts. *Federal Offenders in U.S. District Courts FY 1982*. Washington: Administrative Office of the U.S. Courts, 1983.

Brown, Edward, Timothy Flanagan, and Maureen McLeod, eds. *Sourcebook of Criminal Justice Statistics, 1983*. Washington: Bureau of Justice Statistics, 1984.

Bureau of Justice Statistics. *Federal Drug Law Violators*. Publication no. NCJ–92692. Washington: U.S. Department of Justice, 1984.

Bureau of Prisons. *Bureau of Prisons Annual Statistical Report FY 1981–82*. Washington: Bureau of Prisons, 1982.

Campbell, A. M. G., M. Evans, and J. G. Thompson. "Cerebral Atrophy in Young Cannabis Smokers." *Lancet* 2 (1971): 1219–25.

Clayton, Richard R. and Harwin L. Voss. *Young Men and Drugs in Manhattan: A Causal Analysis*. Monograph no. 59, DHHS Publication no. (ADM) 81–1167. Washington, D.C., 1981.

Commission on Behavioral and Social Sciences and Education. *An Analysis of Marijuana Policy*. Washington: National Academy Press, 1982.

Department of Health and Human Services. *The Health Consequences of Smoking: Nicotine Addiction*. Prepublication edition. Washington: Department of Health and Human Services, 1988.

Drug Abuse Policy Office. *National and International Drug Law Enforcement Strategy*. Washington: National Drug Enforcement Policy Board, 1987.

Drug Abuse Policy Office. *National Strategy for Prevention of Drug Abuse and Drug Trafficking*. Washington: Government Printing Office, 1984.

Drug Enforcement Administration. *Annual Statistical Report FY 1985*. Washington: Drug Enforcement Administration, 1985.

————. *Drug Availability in the United States, 1977–1986*. Washington: Drug Enforcement Administration, 1987.

————. *1984 Domestic Cannabis Eradication/Suppression Program Final Report*. Washington: Drug Enforcement Administration, 1984.

Federal Bureau of Investigation. *Uniform Crime Reports: Crime in the United States, 1986*. Washington: Department of Justice, 1987.

Glantz, Meyer D., ed. *Correlates and Consequences of Marijuana Use*, Research Issues no. 34. Washington: DHHS Publication no. (ADM) 84–1276, 1984.

Griliches, Zvi. "Hedonic Price Indexes Revisited." In *Price Indexes and Quality Change: Studies in New Methods of Measurement*, edited by Zvi Griliches. Cambridge, Mass.: Harvard University Press, 1971.

Grinspoon, Lester, *Marijuana Reconsidered*. Cambridge, Mass.: Harvard University Press, 1971.

Huxley, Matthew. "Criteria for a Socially Sanctionable Drug." *Interdisciplinary Science Reviews* 1 (March 1976): 176–182.

Institute of Medicine. *Marijuana and Health*. Washington: National Academy Press, 1982.

Johnston, Lloyd D., Patrick M. O'Malley, and Jerald G. Bachman. *National Trends in Drug Use and Related Factors Among American High School Students and Young Adults, 1975–1986*. DHHS Publication no. (ADM) 87–1535. Washington: National Institute on Drug Abuse, 1987.

————. *Summary of 1987 Drug Study Results*. Press Release, University of Michigan, 13 January 1988.

Kaplan, John. *The Hardest Drug: Heroin and Public Policy*. Chicago: University of Chicago Press, 1983.

————. *Marijuana: The New Prohibition*. New York: The World Publishing Company, 1971.

Kinsley, Michael. "Glass Houses and Getting Stoned." *Time,* 6 June 1988, 92.

Kleiman, Mark. *Crackdowns: The Effects of Intensive Enforcement on Retail Heroin Dealing*. Kennedy School of Government Working Paper #88–01–11, 9 February 1988.

————. "Drug Enforcement and Organized Crime." In *The Politics and Economics of Organized Crime,* edited by Herbert E. Alexander and Gerald E. Caiden, 67–88. Lexington, Mass.: Lexington Books, 1984.

————. "Marijuana Prohibition Doesn't Pass Gramm-Rudman Test." *The Wall Street Journal,* 8 May 1986, p. 30.

Kolb, Klaus, "The Legalization of Marijuana." Unpublished paper, Policy Analysis Exercise Kennedy School of Government, Harvard University, June 1984.

Lewitt, Eugene M. and Douglas Coate. "The Potential for Using Excise Taxes to Reduce Smoking." Unpublished paper, New Jersey Medical School and National Bureau of Economic Research, 1983.

Marquis, K. H. et al. *Response Errors in Sensitive Topics Surveys: Executive Summary.* RAND Corporation no. R–2710/1-HHS. Santa Monica, Cal.: RAND Corporation, 1981.

Martens, Frederick. "Conflicting Goals in Narcotics Enforcement." Paper presented at the Symposium on Organized Crime and Narcotics, Villanova University, Penn., May 9–11, 1988.

McBay, A. J. and S. M. Owens. "Marijuana and Driving." In *Problems of Drug Dependence, 1980,* edited by L. S. Harris, DHHS Publication no. (ADM) 81–1058, 257–263. Washington: Department of Health and Human Services, 1981.

Mikuriya, Tod and Michael Aldrich. "Cannabis 1988: Old Drug, New Dangers; The Potency Question." In *Journal of Psychoactive Drugs* 20(1) (Winter 1988): 47–55.

Miller, Judith, Ira Cisin, Hilary Gardner-Keaton, Adele Harrel, Philip Wirtz, Herbert Abelson, and Patricia Fishburn. *Highlights from the National Survey on Drug Abuse: 1982.* DHHS Publication no. (ADM) 83–177. Washington, D.C., 1983.

————. *The National Survey on Drug Abuse: Main Findings 1982.* DHHS Publication no. 83–1263. Washington: National Institute on Drug Abuse, 1982.

Mitchell, Thaddeus R. and Robert F. Bell. *Drug Interdiction Operations by the Coast Guard: Summary.* Alexandria, Va.: Center for Naval Analysis, 1980.

Moore, Mark. *Buy and Bust: The Effective Regulation of an Illicit Market in Heroin.* Lexington, Mass.: Lexington Books, 1977.

————. "Limiting the Supply of Drugs to Illicit Markets." *Journal of Drug Issues* 9 (Spring 1979): 291–308.

————. "Policies to Achieve Discrimination in the Effective Price of Heroin." In *American Economic Review* 63 (May 1973): 270–79.

Moore, Mark and Dean Gerstein, eds. *Alcohol and Public Policy: Beyond the Shadow of Prohibition.* Washington: National Academy Press, 1981.

Moore, Mark, Susan R. Estrich, Daniel McGillis, and William Spel-
    man. *Dangerous Offenders: The Elusive Target of Justice*. Cam-
    bridge, Mass.: Harvard University Press, 1984.
Moore, Michael J. and W. Kip Viscusi. "Doubling the Estimated Value
    of Life: Results Using New Occupational Fatality Data." In
    Journal of Policy Analysis and Management 7 (Spring 1988):
    476–490.
Nahas, Gabriel, *Marijuana: Deceptive Weed*. New York: Raven Press,
    1973.
National Institute on Drug Abuse. *Annual Data 1983: Data from the
    Drug Abuse Warning Network (DAWN)*. Series 1, no. 3, DHHS
    Publication no. (ADM) 84–1353. Washington: Department of
    Health and Human Services, 1984.
————. *Annual Data 1986: Data from the Drug Abuse Warning Net-
    work (DAWN)*. Series 1, no. 6, DHHS Publication no. (ADM)
    87–1530. Washington: Department of Health and Human Ser-
    vices, 1987.
————. *National Household Survey on Drug Abuse: Population Esti-
    mates 1985*. DHHS Publication no. (ADM) 87–1537. Washing-
    ton: Department of Health and Human Services, 1987.
————. *Population Projections Based on the National Survey on Drug
    Abuse, 1982*. DHHS Publication no. (ADM) 83–1303. Washing-
    ton, D.C., 1983.
————. *National Household Survey on Drug Abuse: Main Findings
    1985*. DHHS Publication No. (ADM) 88–1586. Washington: De-
    partment of Health and Human Services, 1988.
National Narcotics Intelligence Consumers Committee. *Narcotics In-
    telligence Estimate 1982*. Washington: Drug Enforcement
    Administration, 1983.
————. *Narcotics Intelligence Estimate 1984*. Washington: Drug En-
    forcement Administration, 1985.
————. *Narcotics Intelligence Estimate 1985–86*. Washington: Drug
    Enforcement Administration, 1987.
————. *Narcotics Intelligence Estimate 1987*. Washington: Drug En-
    forcement Administration, 1988.
National Task Force on Cannabis Regulation, *The Regulation and
    Taxation of Cannabis Commerce*. Report. December 1982.
Newcomb, Michael and Peter Bentler. *Consequences of Adolescent
    Drug Use*. Newbury Park, Cal.: Sage Publications, 1988.
Novak, William. *High Culture*. New York: Alfred A. Knopf, 1980.
Organized Crime Drug Enforcement Task Force. *Organized Crime
    Drug Enforcement Task Force Program: Annual Report*. Wash-
    ington: U.S. Department of Justice, March 1984.

Petersen, Robert C. and Richard C. Stillman, eds. *Phencyclidine Abuse: An Appraisal,* Research Monograph no. 21, DHHS Publication no. (ADM) 84–728. Washington: National Institute on Drug Abuse, 1978, reprinted 1984.

Polich, J. Michael, Phyllis L. Ellickson, Peter Reuter, and James P. Kahan. *Strategies for Controlling Adolecent Drug Use.* RAND Corporation Report R–3076-CHF. Santa Monica, Cal.: RAND Corporation, 1984.

Pollin, William. "Drug Abuse U.S.A.: How Serious? How Soluble?" *Issues in Science and Technology* 3 (Winter 1987): 20–27.

Reuter, Peter. "The (Continuing) Vitality of Mythical Numbers." *The Public Interest* 75 (Spring 1984).

———. *Disorganized Crime: The Economics of the Visible Hand.* Cambridge, Mass.: MIT Press, 1983.

———. "Eternal Hope." *The Public Interest* 79 (Spring 1985).

———. "Racketeers as Cartel Organizers." In *The Politics and Economics of Organized Crime,* edited by Herbert E. Alexander and Gerald E. Caiden, 49–66. Lexington, Mass.: Lexington Books, 1984.

———. "La Signification Economique des Marches Illegaux aux Etats-Unis: le Cas de Marijuana," in Edith Archambault and Xavier Greffe (eds), *Les Economies Non Officielles.* Paris: 1984.

———. *The Value of a Bad Reputation: Cartels, Criminals, and Barriers to Entry.* Santa Monica, Cal.: RAND Corporation, 1982.

Reuter, Peter, Gordon Crawford, and Jonathan Cave. *Sealing the Borders: The Effects of Increased Military Participation in Drug Interdiction.* Santa Monica, Cal.: RAND Corportion, January 1988.

Reuter, Peter and Mark A. R. Kleiman. "Risks and Prices." In *Crime and Justice: An Annual Review of Research,* volume 7, edited by M. Tonry and N. Morris, 289–340. Chicago: University of Chicago Press, 1986.

Schelling, Thomas C. *Choice and Consequence.* Cambridge, Mass.: Harvard University Press, 1984.

———. "The Intimate Contest for Self-Command." *The Public Interest* 60 (Summer 1980): 94–118.

———. "What Is the Business of Organized Crime?" *Journal of Public Law* 20 (1971): 71–84.

Spence, A. Michael. "A Note on the Effects of Pressure in the Heroin Market." Harvard Institute of Economic Research Working Paper 588, November 1977.

U.S. Department of Agriculture Economic Research Service. *Tobacco*

Situation and Outlook Report. Washington: Department of Agriculture, 1987.

U.S. Office of Management and Budget. *Budget of the United States Government FY 1982*. Washington: U.S. Office of Management and Budget.

————. *Budget of the United States Government FY 1984* Washington: U.S. Office of Management and Budget, 1984.

————. *Budget of the United States Government FY 1988*. Washington: U.S. Office of Management and Budget, 1988.

Viscusi, W. Kip. *Risk by Choice*. Cambridge, Mass.: Harvard University Press, 1983.

Warner, Roger. *The Invisible Hand: The Marijuana Business*. New York: Beech Tree Books, 1986.

Young, Francis L. *Opinion and Recommended Ruling, Findings of Fact, Conclusions of Law and Decision of Administrative Law Judge in the Matter of Marijuana Rescheduling Petition*. United States Department of Justice, Drug Enforcement Administration: Docket no. 86–22, 6 September 1988.

Index

ABOUT THE AUTHOR

MARK KLEIMAN is in the Program in Criminal Justice Policy and Management at Harvard Univeristy.